To

Mina Becker Buys

and her great granddaughter

Rachel Mina Buys

About the Author

Christian J. Buys has written five previous books on Colorado history: *Historic Leadville in Rare Photographs and Drawings, Historic Telluride in Rare Photographs, Illustrations of Historic Colorado, Historic Aspen in Rare Photographs — Featuring the Journals of Charles S. Armstrong,* and *The Lost Journals of Charles S. Armstrong — From Arkport, New York to Aspen, Colorado, 1867-1894.* Buys has also written numerous articles in psychology, nautical archaeology, and other aspects of Colorado history.

Awarded Fulbright Scholarships to Egypt and Malaysia, Buys and his family have traveled extensively. Currently he is a professor of psychology at Mesa State College in Grand Junction, Colorado. Visits to Telluride and hikes in the surrounding mountains remain high on his priority list.

TELLURIDE

By Christian J. Buys

WESTERN REFLECTIONS
PUBLISHING COMPANY ®

Montrose, Colorado

© 2003 Christian J. Buys
All rights reserved in whole or in part.

ISBN 1-890437-83-2

Library of Congress Control Number: 2003102288

Cover photo: Cable for Nellie Mine Tramway, Telluride, Colorado
(Courtesy P. David Smith)
Cover and text design by Laurie Goralka Design

First Edition
Printed in the United States of America

Western Reflections Publishing Company®
219 Main Street
Montrose, CO 81401
www.westernreflectionspub.com

Table Of Contents

TELLURIDE REGIONAL MAP

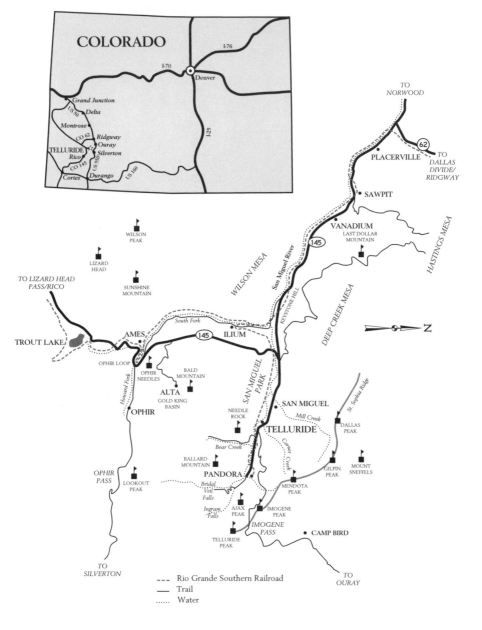

UPPER SAN MIGUEL MINING DISTRICT

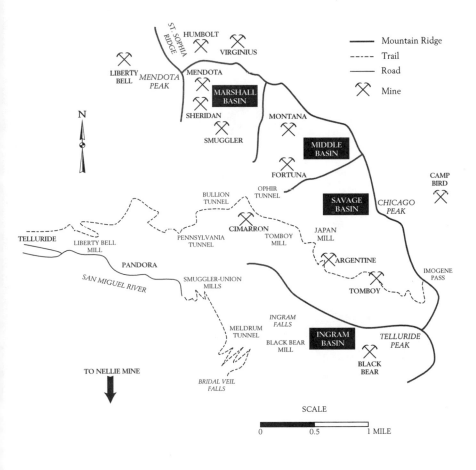

CHAPTER ONE

Before Telluride

Telluride sprang to life in San Miguel Park, one of the most picturesque alpine valleys in the West. Nearly six miles long and half a mile wide, the park is traversed by the San Miguel River. In spring the river's muddy-brown water churns through an emerging abundance of brightly colored wild flowers. By summer its hearty turquoise swells splash over smooth boulders, complementing the greenish hues of conifers and salt cedars that intermittently crowd its banks. Come fall the San Miguel's sky-blue water courses more slowly through a cornucopia of oranges, reds, and yellows created by patches of high-altitude aspen and scrub oak. Skittish mule deer lower their heads to drink its bracing liquid while trout flash by. During winter the icy blue river slows, meandering among cornices of windblown snow that blankets the entire six-mile-long flat.

If this splendid kaleidoscope of alpine seasons is not enough to savor, all one has to do is stand anywhere in the small town of modern Telluride and simply look up. What greets the eye is so magnificent, so inspiring that it confirms the faithfuls' belief in a beneficent god, heightens agnostics' sense of wonder, and causes atheists to marvel. For there above them — closely hugging San Miguel Park — loom massive mountains whose lofty white peaks caress the brilliant azure skies. Already light-headed from the high altitude, visibly awed tourists often stop and stare at the nearby scenery, blocking the sidewalks in downtown Telluride. Who can blame them? Mainly they gaze east, where bulging creeks rush out of high basins, plummet hundreds of feet, then vanish into a slender silver mist. Close by, enigmatic dark lines zigzag up the impossibly precipitous mountains. Ascending one way, then another into the gray heights, these threadlike traces become fainter, ultimately disappearing into huge basins surrounded by snow-whitened peaks. It takes time, sometimes days, for the mind to appreciate fully this awe-inspiring scene. After all, Telluride's towering mountain backdrop combined with its pristine alpine-park setting has few rivals on earth for sheer natural beauty.

The zigzag lines hold the key to this book. They are not geologic faults. Rather, those distinct lines are switchbacks in hair-raising trails dynamited and hammered out in the late nineteenth century — each inch providing a precipitous path to a fortune, or so the builders hoped. Telluride, in fact, came into existence because of the mineral-rich ores entombed for eons in the massive stone mountains that nearly surround it. That Native Americans first inhabited the park, enjoying its rich bounty for centuries, hardly seemed to matter when word of the new strike spread throughout the United States in the 1870s. There was no stopping the mineral-hungry hordes. It was neither the first time, nor would it be the last, that avarice spiced with adventure resulted in the unlawful and unethical displacement of one people by another.

In the early 1860s the Utes must have watched, wondering, as the Charles Baker party snaked its way over present-day Ophir Pass into their treasured alpine parks. They had not seen strangers like these in their homeland since the few fur-traders whom they had forced out decades earlier. Baker's party didn't stay long in the valley (if, in fact, they reached San Miguel Park), so the Utes could not have known that this disheveled band of Anglo-American prospectors was a harbinger of a massive wave of humanity that would soon inundate their homeland and drive them away.

The Utes' demise happened fast and unfairly. By 1868 they had signed a treaty with the United States that "granted" them about one-quarter of present-day Western Colorado, including the — unbeknownst at the time — mineral-rich San Juan Mountains. By 1873, however, the mining interests became so strong that they reluctantly ceded four million acres of the San Juan Mountains to the United States for a perpetual yearly annuity of $25,000, mostly in the form of goods. Finally, during the late summer in 1881, the few Utes remaining in present-day Western Colorado embarked on a forced exodus to Utah Territory. Most of them could not bear to look back at their beloved valleys and mountains, now swarming with mineral-hungry intruders.

Earlier, in 1872, Linnard Remine and a few companions — possibly the first men to enter the San Miguel Valley since the fur traders — illegally had started placer mining on the Ute Reservation. Long-time Telluride resident Martin G. Wenger, who as a young boy knew Remine, recounts that Remine journeyed into the remote Telluride region "as a result of a fight incident in the mining camp of Creede. [Either Remine or Wenger are mistaken, Creede did not exist until 1889.] Someone had jumped his mining claim there and in the following fight Remine thought he had killed the man. He left Creede and worked his way to [the] present town of Delta." Later, Remine learned that he had not killed the man, so he decided to search for gold in the San Juans. Thus, Remine led a small band of his friends over the longer and lower present-day Dallas Divide around Last Dollar Mountain. Then he hiked along the San Miguel River into San Miguel Park. There, in the early 1870s, he and his companions cut "enough grass to feed their trail-weary packstock" (Lavender, 1987). Remine told Wenger that they "started placer mining and they each made about $15.00 a day panning for gold" (Wenger, 1987).

Thoughts of the resulting devastation to the Utes' way of life did not enter the prospectors' minds. Rather, they carefully cultivated a friendship with the powerful Utes who came each summer and fall to hunt and fish in game-rich San Miguel Park. With his primitive cabin as his base, Linnard Remine staked several claims and ran trap lines. Years later Remine said the Utes told him of early Spanish mining activity in the park. Coupled with the unconfirmed rumors of the "discovery of old Spanish tools on a certain vein opening" in nearby mountains, Remine's report has fueled rumors of hidden Spanish treasure and lost mines ever since.

It is no rumor that the government-sponsored Hayden Survey group mapped the San Miguel Valley in 1874, or that in 1875 John Fallon somehow scaled a spectacular 13,000-foot-high craggy granite barrier near St. Sophia Ridge. Then Fallon managed to make it down into Marshall Basin from the east. He wasn't interested in panning for a few nuggets. He sought the mother lode. Fallon staked out five claims in Marshall Basin in October 1875. Mining-town myth holds that this first shipment of ore to Silverton, where he officially filed his claims, put $10,000 into his pockets. The precise value of that original ore carried by Fallon's small string of burros doesn't really matter. What matters is that Fallon had found a rich deposit of gold ore. Another Colorado Territory mineral rush was on.

We should remind ourselves that when Fallon and other prospectors struck out toward the San Miguel Park, there was nothing in the way of "civilization" in this region. Prospectors were basically on their own — with few sources of food or shelter. All their camping supplies, prospecting equipment, and most of their food had to be carried in or packed on mules. Their very lives depended on primitive, heavy equipment and clothing that any modern mountain backpacker would consider wholly inadequate and downright dangerous. One unfortunate slip by mule or man also meant trouble, big trouble. If a prospector didn't plummet to his death off some narrow rock-strewn trail, a sprained ankle, or worse yet a major broken bone, meant certain agony and possibly death. They simply could not afford to become ill. Further, many prospectors came from east of the Mississippi and nothing in the East could have prepared them for the sheer scale of the West. Their first look at the Rockies must have taken them aback. For there before their unbelieving eyes loomed the most powerful and forbidding geological phenomenon they had ever seen. Once they crossed into one of the basins above San Miguel Valley they might as well have been on another planet. It was that remote and threatening to anyone but the most adventuresome.

In spite of these daunting obstacles, between 1860 and 1880 thousands of fortune seekers spread out across present-day Colorado. Viewed from above, this throng must have looked like an army of starving ants slowly surging into nearly impenetrable terrain. What happened at Telluride occurred all over the Rocky Mountains. At first, small groups of prospectors groped their way along the unexplored contours of the Rocky

Mountains. If they struck gold or silver, like Fallon did, they stayed where they found it. A trickle of prospectors soon followed. Within months the trickle metamorphosed into a continuous line of fortune seekers and adventurers. Soon each discovery site became a thickly populated pocket of frenetic mining and mining-support activity. Once every inch of ground, or so it seemed, had been claimed, and once the mining camp started to mature into a town, restless souls seeking new discoveries headed over the next mountain range. So it was with the first prospectors to make the arduous journey into the distant San Juans and the beautiful San Miguel Valley.

Thus, by the summer of 1875 Remine and his companions were no longer alone. Over 300 men had invaded the pristine San Miguel Valley to work the gravel along the San Miguel River, while many others feverishly scoured the mountains. Meanwhile, Fallon staked five claims in Marshall Basin: Emerald, Tripple, Sheridan, Ansborough, and Fallon. The Sheridan became the shining star.

The following year, in the area below Fallon's claims in Marshall Basin, the Pandora Mine (eventually a small mill town) was staked out by James Carpenter and Thomas Lowthian on the eastern edge of San Miguel Park. Also in 1876, according to Colorado historian Robert Brown:

> One J. B. Ingram was prospecting in the [Marshall] [B]asin. It occurred to him at the time that the Union and Sheridan claims exceeded their legal allowance. Taking his own measurements, he discovered that both had about five hundred feet of land that was not legally theirs. Putting down his own stake upon the surplus ground, he named his property [boldly] the Smuggler. This incredible bit of good fortune resulted in one of the region's richest mines.

Then W. L. Cornett discovered the promising Liberty Bell gold mine high at the head of Cornet Creek (named after him, but spelled with one less "t"). News of these phenomenal discoveries in the San Juans spread fast. By 1877, the rush was really on.

Williams' Tourists' Guide (1877) quickly got in on the act. "Until September, 1872," the guide's author wrote, "the entire section known as 'the San Juan Country' was part of the Ute Indian reservation. At that time the Indian title was extinguished, and the country thrown open to settlement." Of yet-to-be-named Telluride, *Williams' Tourists' Guide* wrote:

> The San Miguel placer mines [present-day Telluride], twenty-five miles west of Silverton, located on the San Miguel River (which in Spanish signifies St. Michael) attracted considerable attention during 1875. Prospecting has not been done sufficiently to settle the character and richness of the district. The gold so far taken out is coarse, and has yielded ten to fifty cents to the pan. By going to

bedrock it is believed that richer and larger deposits will be found. There will be, no doubt, a thorough investigation made of the river bed the coming season, and probably another mining excitement. The altitude is much lower than the silver regions of the San Juans. The climate is very mild. The valley is well-timbered and the soil rich.

Williams'Tourists'Guide was one of the most popular guides to the San Juans. (Author's collection)

The reliability of such guides suffered because they were often penned by persons who had never been to the destinations they described.

In 1877 several railroads advertised passage to the San Juan mining region in, among others, Williams' popular tourist guides. Each railroad company promised comfortable and punctual connections to Denver or Pueblo where they could board the Denver & Rio Grande Railway (D&RGRy) to its "Western Terminus [end of the tracks], where all the San Juan Freighting and Outfitting is done." The D&RGRy's ad promised "No delays on the Route" to "The Best and Richest Mining District in the World."

Gold-hungry enthusiasts eager to believe such propaganda undoubtedly trusted the guidebook's weather reports as well:

The climate of the San Juan is one of the finest in the world. The pure, bracing mountain air expands the lungs, gives vivacity, energy, and robust health. Malaria is unknown. The temperate is moderate. The winters are not more severe than in other portions of the State, and even thus far the winters of 1875-6-7 have been milder in the San

Sometimes artists fabricated images of mining in the San Juans. (Author's collection)

Juan country than else-where of same altitude in Colorado.

Idyllic drawings of mining scenes, combined with the railroads' propaganda, provided the impetus for thousands of people to head for the San Juans. For example, this cozy-looking stagecoach travels past numerous miners panning their fortunes in a crisp, clean mountain environment. One of the miners waves a friendly hat at the passengers, as though beckoning them to join him. Water pours from a long sluice — undoubtedly sparkling with gold. In the background surrealistic cliffs reach out to touch each other across a narrow canyon.

Placer mining could be highly destructive to the environment. (Reprinted from **Telluride and San Miguel County,** *1894)*

Realistic drawings of the scenery around pres-ent-day Telluride. (Courtesy of P. David Smith)

The early guidebooks could not, however, exaggerate the beauty of the San Juans. Drawings in a *Harper's Weekly* (June 11, 1887) show some of the high country near present-day Telluride described by the *Williams' Tourists' Guide* as "a scene of beauty the imagination cannot depict."

Once the miners had panned out the surface gold in the San Miguel River, destructive hydraulic mining (washing the ore-bearing gravel out of the hillsides) started in earnest in 1877. Keystone Hill, at the top of the cascades (about three miles west of present-day Telluride), had the most active hydraulic mining after "the Wheeler and Kimball Ditch was completed to carry water to the claims" (Brown, 1968).

Sam Blair ran one of the earliest sawmills in the region. It provided wood for several of the homes in San Miguel, the first settlement in the valley. Many of the homes and businesses in Columbia (two miles east of San Miguel) were also constructed with wood from Blair's mill on Mill Creek. Columbia (present-day Telluride) was incorporated by the unanimous decision of all twenty-eight voters on July 18, 1878.

Even today sources differ in their accounts of this early mining community's schizophrenic journey to be named Telluride. Most accounts agree that San Miguel, soon to be San Miguel City, was first settled about two miles west of Columbia during 1875 and 1876 (near present-day Society Turn.) In 1878 Columbia sprang up about two miles east of San Miguel City. Located closer to the mines, it would soon supplant San Miguel City (population "5 women and 200 men" by 1880) in significance and size. Yet in 1885 the map supplied with Crofutt's popular

Telluride (Columbia) in the mid-1880s consisted mainly of wood frame structures. (T. McKee photo: Denver Public Library, Western History Department)

Grip-Sack Guide of Colorado (1885) shows only "San Miguel" (without "City"). Columbia is also shown, but it appears in conjunction with the settlement of "Folsom."

It turns out that Folsom was originally called Newport, which was located immediately east of Columbia. In time Folsom became Pandora (named after an early claim), where the great mills were built. Most of the confusion, however, hinged on the location of a proper post office — a major source of pride for any mining-town community. Trouble was, the name "Columbia" was already taken by a California town and the abbreviated "Col" and "Cal" were just too hard to distinguish. Yet the Washington postal authorities refused to change the post office name from Columbia to Telluride, as some of the town's people wished ("Telluride" was taken from the nonmetallic element tellurium which is virtually nonexistent in the region). In the early 1880s the post office of Telluride (the name preferred by the majority of locals) was actually transferred to the town of Folsom. So people from Telluride had to go to Folsom to pick up their mail.

"Who straightened out Telluride's identity is unknown, but on December 13, 1880, the post office, Telluride, was returned to its original location, although the town itself still clung to the name Columbia" (Lavender, 1987). Mercifully, on June 4, 1887, Telluride officially became "Telluride," a name — then and now — unique in America.

By the mid-1880s Columbia consisted mainly of wood frame structures, with the exception of the newly built brick courthouse on Colorado Avenue. The American House Hotel, a large rectangular building that faced north on Colorado Avenue, was the dominate structure in town.

CHAPTER TWO

The Early Years

During the early 1880s, people backed by money and people with money started Telluride on a course followed by many mountain boomtowns. Thanks to capitalists willing to risk large sums, within a few years some of the high mines in the nearby mountains started paying off. With cash flowing into Telluride, businesses soon crowded together in crude structures astride Telluride's main street, wooden houses started to replace tents and log cabins, schools welcomed their first students, lawyers poured into town, and a volunteer fire department quickly formed. There were no churches. While most locals welcomed these first signs of civilization, a few probably preferred the mining camp to remain the way it was — with mining, bawdiness, and booze dominating the tenor of the town. Still, because of its remote location and the formidable mountain barriers, it would take several years (until the railroad arrived) for Telluride to reach the pinnacle of its mining-days glory.

Unlike many early San Juan mining towns, Telluride had a spacious main street. Even today temporary parking for deliveries is allowed in the middle of Colorado Avenue. Joseph Collier set up his tripod and camera facing east to record this rare image of many of Telluride's (technically

Although labeled "Telluride," this early photo shows what the post office technically called "Columbia." Notice, too, the name "Telluride House." (Denver Public Library, Western History Department)

Columbia's) earliest businesses. On the south side of Colorado Avenue, Denison's grocery store stands next to S. R. Fitgarralo's law office. Farther down are Tryan's Hardware, Oderfeld's General Merchandise shop, and a meat market. Across Colorado Avenue are the Telluride House, Stewart's Hardware, and the American House (the tallest structure), a familiar point of reference in early panoramas of the mining camp. Telluride's infamous post office, a bakery, and a grocery store stand farther down the block.

Two men and a boy on the boardwalk under Denison's sign stopped to stare intently at the camera, as did several men from across the street. The man at the left-center of the photograph continued to cross the street, causing his image to blur. Several pack burros gathered on Telluride's dirt thoroughfare are most likely waiting to ascend the steep trails to the mines.

During the 1870s and 1880s freighters such as Dave Wood comprised the life line to Telluride and the mines. Without them, no one in the mining camp would have prospered. Two of Wood's daughters, Francis and Dorothy, recount, "Wood played an historic part in opening up the western slope of the Great Divide. His huge freight wagons hauled in food, machinery, dynamite, coal — everything needed at the mines."

Wood's canvas-covered wagons carried the names of the places they served. "Telluride" appears on the second wagon in this unusual tandem. The flat terrain and low hills in the background indicate the photograph was taken near Montrose. In another image, Dave Wood, standing beside

Dave Wood's freight wagons were seen all over the San Juans. (Courtesy of P. David Smith)

Dave Wood's main office is shown here at Montrose, Colorado. (Walker and Southwest Collection, Center of Southwest Studies, Fort Lewis College)

his buggy, is shown operating his many-tentacled freight business from Montrose, Colorado. The huge livery barn and corrals accommodated over 100 head of stock. Included in this count were twenty mule teams, all matched. Wood's "Transportation Lines" prospered, grossing over $150,000 during three months in 1882.

"He freighted over roads that were scarcely more than trails, and where there was no road at all he built one. Where there were no towns he helped build those, too, and added his freight stations and warehouses" (Wood and Wood, 1977). In fact, Dave Wood spent $30,000 to have a private freighting road built across Horsefly Mesa to Leonard in order to avoid some of the worst of the rough miles between Montrose and Telluride as well as severe problems caused along the route by floods. No one is certain why he named it "The Magnolia Route."

In early 1881 Dolores County, which included Telluride and Silverton, splintered away from the unwieldy Ouray County. Two years later the state legislature created another smaller county, San Miguel, in which Telluride remains.

In downtown Telluride mining-support businesses like W. B. Van Atta catered to the miners' and their families' needs. What few people realize is that there was a better chance of accumulating a small fortune in business than in prospecting. The truth is that very few fortune seekers ever struck it rich while mining in Colorado Territory, or anywhere else in the West. Abysmal odds never seemed to faze the glassy-eyed hordes of money-hungry people. Worse, even if prospectors discovered a rich min-

Merchants like W. B. Van Atta often made much more money than local prospectors. (Reprinted from Telluride and San Miguel County, *1894)*

eral deposit in the early days, it would not have made them rich. Having the Midas touch was not enough. It took thousands of dollars in labor and capital to extract precious mineral from the ore in which it was embedded. Before a prospector saw a dime, unless someone came along and bought the claim, his ore had to mined, transported to a smelter (a dangerous, arduous, expensive task in mountainous terrain), crushed, refined, melted into bullion, and sent off to buyers hundreds, sometimes thousands, of miles away. Shipping bullion in bulk out of the high basins near Telluride was impossible until the smelters fired up in the mid-1880s and the railroad arrived in 1890. Yet this clearly did not deter thousands of eager and optimistic fortune seekers.

Meanwhile, business entrepreneurs in early Telluride earned money, big money. W. B. Van Atta opened his business on the northwest corner of Colorado Avenue and Pine Street in 1883. He promoted his store as the "Up-to-date Outfitter," offering a "complete line of clothing for men and women, along with a fine assortment of yard goods." Van Atta quickly became one of the more important businessmen in Telluride. Stories circulated that he once sold $2,000 worth of merchandise in a single evening. All credit had to be settled each month, or a 2% interest charge per month would be assessed.

Another successful businessman, Charles F. Painter, served as Telluride's first mayor, first county clerk, and publisher of the first newspaper, *The Journal.* By 1889 he also oversaw a successful insurance, loan, and abstract company that operated for several decades. These were all strictly family

The Painter family posed on "Chair Rock" near the high school. (Courtesy of Bill Mahoney)

businesses. Painter's talented grandson, David Lavender, became a prolific writer.

There is no mention of a public school in an early description of Telluride: "Seat of San Miguel County, on the upper San Miguel River, surrounded by high mountains covered with timber and filled with rich minerals; altitude, 8,410 feet. It contains one bank, stores of all kinds, several hotels, one 20 and one 40 stamp mill, one weekly newspaper — the News, and a population of about 1,400, most of whom are engaged in mining" (*Grip-Sack Guide of Colorado*, 1885).

Actually the Telluride (then still called Columbia) area school district was formed four years earlier (August 10, 1881) in a portion of Ouray County. Lillian Blair served as the first teacher and held classes in W. A. Taylor's house, which was located where St. Patrick's Church now stands. In 1883 the people of Telluride built a wooden schoolhouse for $3,000 to be "replaced by a brick one which later housed the town hall." Currently mounted on the town hall, the school bell serves as a fire alarm bell.

Portrait photographs, like the one shown here, proved especially popular in mining towns and show that not every resident of Telluride was involved with mining as an occupa-

L. Emery was a Telluride cowboy. (Denver Public Library, Western History Department)

tion. In this photograph, L. Emery of Telluride poses before a painted, stone block wall backdrop typical for the period. Real dried grass covers the floor. Emery's 44-40 caliber, 1873 Winchester rifle can be identified by the distinct line on the breech. Since this Winchester model was about forty-two inches long, Emery must have been short. His leather chaps afforded his legs protection from bushes and helped keep them warm in winter. This style of chaps carried the name "shotgun chaps" because of its stovepipe shape. Obviously, Emery earned his living as a cowboy.

Imagine the confusion and controversy that James P. Redick, Telluride's first "postmaster and newsdealer," faced until Columbia finally changed its name to Telluride in 1887. According to long-time resident Alta Cassietto, Redick's daughter had the distinction of being the first child born in Telluride (although it was still officially named Columbia). Alta Cassietto served as Telluride's postmaster from 1934 to 1970. Her parents gave her the name of the mine where she was born — Alta.

Telluride's second postmaster, John B. Frasher, also served as county treasurer. His sorrow over the unexpected death of his beloved wife was too much for him to bear. Frasher walked down to the Lone Tree Cemetery and took his own life on her grave.

During the early 1880s the Telluride mining region grew steadily. What little flat ground could be found at lower elevations quickly blossomed into small multicultural, mining-support communities. The dirt streets of mining camps like Ames, Rico, Ophir, Sawpit, and Placerville teemed with freight wagons and strings of heavily loaded animals bound for the high-country mines. Crude boardwalks allowed people to avoid the deep mud. Several false-front buildings, including the ubiquitous mining-camp saloons, bordered the muddy thoroughfares.

In 1885 Ames, located about five miles south of Telluride, was described in a popular tourists guide as, "a mining camp on the San Miguel River, where are located smelting works and about 200 people." Ames blossomed near a site that would soon become a famous railroad loop.

Numerous early photographs featured loaded pack burros ready to begin their arduous climb to the high country mines. This grouping of burros was gathered on Ames's main street, while men handling the wagon wait for the beasts of burden to move aside. One wonders about the profession of the woman peering from the second story window. Canvas ore bags are slung across the backs of the two burros closest to the camera. Packing trail animals constituted an art that not everyone could master.

In the late 1880s the mining camp of Rico, south of Lizard Head Pass, grew faster than any other camp in the region, including Telluride. "Seat of Dolores County, [Rico] is a mining town of much promise. It is situated on the east fork of the Dolores River, in a beautiful little valley, at the junction of Silver Creek, 35 miles from Silverton — 'as the bird

Pack burros were known as "the ships of the mountains." (Denver Public Library, Western History Department)

would fly' [and about equidistant from Telluride]. Population, 1,500. Altitude, 8,653 feet [a modern highway sign shows the elevation as 8,827 feet]. Rico has two banks, stores, hotels, restaurants, and saloons of all kinds, with churches, and schools, together with four smelting works" (*Grip-Sack Guide of Colorado*, 1885).

The interior of an unidentified Telluride saloon. (Denver Public Library, Western History Department)

Still, throughout the 1880s, Telluride reigned supreme among the mining camps in the region. By 1887 Telluride boasted numerous booming businesses, a population that swelled to over 2,000 (including the surrounding mines), ten saloons, but still no church. The "openness" of the rich camp may be why Butch Cassidy and his gang picked Telluride to be one of their robbery targets. In the summer of 1889, they relieved the San Miguel County Bank of its monthly miners' payroll money — approximately $24,000, which was never recovered.

The "Wild Bunch" pose in their fancy clothes. The "Sundance Kid" is on the left and Butch Cassidy is on the right. (Telluride Historical Museum)

A posse headed by none other than the owner of the bank, Lucien Nunn (see pages 20 - 23), took off in hot pursuit of Butch and his Wild Bunch:

> *The race was close. This was evident a few months later when the carcasses of four horses were found still tied to a tree. They had been left for relay, but the outlaws had been crowded into a different getaway route and were unable to pick them up. The robbers did rest a bit at Trout Lake but disappeared as soon as the posse got too close* (Fetter and Fetter, 1979).

CHAPTER THREE

San Juan Boom Town

T he 1890s was Telluride's finest decade. The arrival of the Rio
Grande Southern Railroad signaled the start of Telluride's first sus-
tained economic boom — it would wait nearly a century for another.
More people, supplies, and mining equipment rode behind the smoke-
and-cinder spewing engines that chugged their way over Dallas Divide.
By 1891 the narrow-gauge tracks extended south over rugged Lizard
Head Pass to booming Rico. By early 1892 the first Rio Grande Southern
train rolled into Durango. Now more ore from the San Miguel Mining
District could be transported faster, easier, and cheaper to Durango's
belching smelters.

*Snuggled beneath snow-covered peaks, Telluride awaits the coming of winter in
1890. In the foreground Rio Grande Southern freight cars wait on sidetracks
extending on both sides of the depot. (Reprinted from* Telluride and San Miguel
County, *1894)*

As United States troops dismantled Fort Crawford south of Montrose,
Colorado, mason workers in Telluride laid the first brick of the Sheridan
Hotel. That same year 1,500 workers started construction of the Rio
Grande Southern from Ridgway to Telluride. By November 23, 1891, the
first locomotive chugged into the bustling camp, signaling the beginning of
Telluride's enviable position as a San Juan boom town.

Prosperity truly rode to Telluride on the rails of the Rio Grande Southern in 1891. The one name that will always be synonymous with the construction of the Rio Grande Southern is Russian-born Otto Mears:

> By 1889 Mears had connected much of southwestern Colorado with his roads. Included in his accomplishments was the spectacular road from Ouray to Silverton via Red Mountain, much of which was cut out of the solid rock of the Uncompahgre Canyon. On October 30 he formed the Rio Grande Southern Railroad with a group of prominent citizens that included the governor, and he set his sights on a project that would reach Telluride. The railroad was to be narrow-gauge, and the work would be done by the Rio Grande Southern Construction Company. To finance the venture Mears sold a total of $9,020,000 worth of stocks and bonds in the company. Telluride in fact would be but part of a great line that ran down through Rico, Dolores, and Mancos, to connect Ridgway with Durango (Fetter and Fetter, 1979).

A Rio Grande Southern sightseeing train in the 1940s edges out onto "The Loop." (Denver Public Library, Western History Department)

Mear's railroad to Telluride was the last major narrow-gauge railroad to be constructed in Colorado. Not only did the Rio Grande Southern traverse some of Colorado's most spectacular mountains, it included the famous Ophir Loop between Telluride and Rico, which ranks among the premier railroad building feats of the late nineteenth century. An awed contemporary wrote:

> The difficulties of mountain ascent surmounted and overcome by engineering skill so that a path is made for the puffing steam engine to pull its trail of commerce up the rugged, almost perpendicular sides and over their summits, has in Ophir Loop a marvelous exhi-

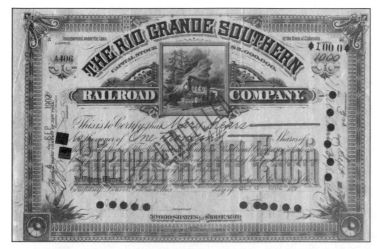

These shares of Rio Grande Southern stock were made out to Mary Mears, Otto's wife. (Courtesy of P. David Smith)

bition. To see it is to be confounded and enchanted by its magnificent grandeur, and marvelous confirmation of the triumphs of engineering skill in this our day and generation. The illustration [below] which accompanies this article is but a faint expression of what you must realize by a trip over the Loop by rail" (Telluride and San Miguel County, 1894).

With the coming of the Rio Grande Southern, Dave Wood's business-stationery vignette featuring stage and freight stock soon gave way, figuratively and literally, to the steam engine vignette on the stock certificate shown above.

By 1891 a Colorado State Business Directory credits booming Telluride with over ninety business houses, including hardware stores, blacksmith shops, jewelry stores, planning mills and photographic galleries, boot and shoe stores, drug stores, grocery stores, livery stables, barber and bath shops, a paint shop, millinery store, fruit and confectionery store, furniture store, feed store, brewery, laundries, one church, and several saloons. Also listed were the addresses of numerous lawyers, doctors, assayers, and insurance men.

Early illustration of the Ophir Loop. (Reprinted from Telluride and San Miguel County, 1894*)*

The distinctive rock formation in the background gave Lizard Head Pass its name. (Courtesy of P. David Smith)

Yet Telluride's boom, even with the arrival of the Rio Grande Southern, would have fizzled were it not for the genius and pluck of a diminutive entrepreneur, Lucien Lucius Nunn. It is difficult to conceive how so little fame has accrued to Nunn, who catapulted Telluride and the San Juans into the age of electricity. In fact, during the early 1890s, this Telluride resident formed the center of a scientific whirlwind that swept its way across Colorado, the United States, and the world.

It all had to do with supplying power to the mines. Steam power had served the San Juan mining industry well until the mid-1880s when the adjacent forests began to disappear as miners cut thousands of trees for fuel, lumber, and the mines. It became cheaper to have coal packed in by burros at forty to fifty dollars per ton than to transport wood from more distant locations. Steam-powered machinery became expensive to operate, as did the huge boilers at the mines. Imagine a month fuel bill — even now — of $2,500. Many of the mines located in remote regions failed because of the prohibitively high fuel costs. Indeed, profits at most mines in the Telluride region nose-dived.

Lucien Nunn was a small man who did big things. (Courtesy of Arlene Reid)

Enter Lucien Nunn. Successful, tormented, and largely ignored by history, Lucien Nunn cut a formidable path through Telluride. He also almost single-handedly saved the San Juan region's mining industry. Reared on a farm in Ohio, his collegiate career began with a brief and informal sojourn to study law at Leipzig and Goettingen Universities in Germany. He returned to the United States for further study in a Boston law office and attended an occasional lecture at Harvard Law School in 1879. Attracted by visions of wealth in the West, he arrived in Leadville, Colorado, along with thousands of other fortune seekers in 1880. His brief stint in Leadville was not successful. The Pacific Grotto Restaurant he opened in the rear of a gambling house in town failed. He decided to settle in Tombstone, Arizona. But threats of Indian hostilities in Tombstone changed his mind. Instead, he moved to Durango, Colorado, where he opened another Pacific Grotto Restaurant. Once again Nunn's efforts as a connoisseur restauranteur floundered.

So in 1881, in his twenty-eighth year, he disconsolately arrived in Telluride. But this time he succeeded. Despite his tiny five-feet-one-inch frame, he had also done considerable construction and fine carpentry work in Leadville and Durango. Drawing upon this exemplary carpentry work, considerable law skills, and Napoleonic drive, he pushed himself to the top of the Telluride business world by 1888. His bachelor mansion with a fine study and zinc-lined bathtub was the largest in town. A sixteen-stall stable held his favorite steeds which he expertly rode. Two guest homes made visitors comfortable.

By 1890 Nunn held controlling interest, with William Story, in the only bank in San Miguel County (which the Wild Bunch had robbed in 1889), three of the best store buildings on Colorado Avenue, and small interests in several mines, including the Gold King situated south of Telluride above Alta Lakes. But soon Nunn, like other mine owners in the region, began to fret over the high cost of fuel. Nunn, however, decided to do something about it.

Today, alternating current is a familiar electrical concept. But in 1890, when Nunn decided to erect a high-voltage alternating-current generating station at Ames, about five miles south of Telluride, few people had ever heard of it. In fact, with two notable exceptions — Nikola Tesla who had conceived of alternating current and George Westinghouse who was impressed by this young Croatian touched with genius — no one had faith in it. Further, this untested electric phenomenon had never been used for commercial purposes. Thomas Edison called the concept of alternating current splendid, but "utterly impractical." Nunn disagreed. He felt this odd-sounding phenomenon of "alternating current" held the key to solving the region's exorbitantly high fuel costs.

Rushing water from the San Miguel River was diverted into hoses in the small, crude power station. There it came blasting out of small nozzles, supplying the power to turn two six-foot-diameter Pelton water wheels belted

The birth of modern-day electricity near Telluride affected the very fiber of our modern culture. (Fort Lewis College, Center of Southwest Studies)

to a Westinghouse generator. Under the careful supervision of Paul Nunn (Lucien's brother), a new Westinghouse single-phase generator, primitive by today's standards, and an experimental motor designed by Tesla were finally in place as the winter of 1890-91 reached its frigid peak. Two transmission lines of bare copper wire were strung for almost three miles from the floor of the valley to the 12,000-foot altitude of the Gold King Mine. Porcelain insulators atop Western Union cross-arms held the wire. The $700 cost was one percent of the construction cost of a direct-current line.

In early spring of 1891, when Nunn was thirty-seven years old, all was ready. The farmers and ranchers who lived downstream from the Ames plant worried about the pending start-up. "Essences" and "life forces" of the stream, they claimed, would be sucked from the water, its salubrious strength compromised. In an era when transportation and speed were judged against the standard of a good mule or a fast horse, supplying power in alternating directions in mysterious copper lines at 186,000 miles per second was simply too much for them to accept.

Suddenly, or so it seemed after such colossal investments of time, energy, and hopes, Nunn threw the switch. Those present, no doubt, gasped and jumped back as a brilliant arc shot six feet into the air. In less time than a blink of an eye the Gold King had electrical power to oper-ate hoists and ore crushers, economical power that was to prove the sal-vation of the mining industry and transform the commercial application of electricity forever.

The familiarity with which we perceive electricity today understandably detracts from an appreciation for its controversial development and use in America during the 1880s and 1890s. Few other eras in history have been privileged to see the birth and maturation of a phenomenon — electricity — which was to affect the very fiber of human culture. And all this in tiny Ames, just below Telluride.

By the mid-1890s, with a bustling population approaching 3,000, downtown Telluride thrived. Several new businesses blossomed along the dirt main street. The main street businesses included, among others, the Cosmopolitan Saloon, a barbershop, gambling hall, stationery store, drugstore, and jewelry store. The First National Bank building stood across North Fir Street. The New Sheridan Hotel and the San Miguel County

Men stand in suits on the boardwalk. A covered delivery wagon is almost obscured by the long mule pack train. (Denver Public Library, Western History Department)

The Sheridan (Hotel) building exemplified Telluride's sturdy business buildings built during the 1890s. (Reprinted from Telluride and San Miguel County, *1894)*

Courthouse were at the west end of main street. A thick layer of coarse stone had been carefully spread along the center of the atypically wide Colorado Avenue, giving a very finished look to the town.

The 1890s proved to be a banner decade for selling merchandise in Telluride:

> *All lines of merchandising are well represented by staunch, enterprising business houses, both wholesale and retail. There are, perhaps, more than a dozen houses that carry stock aggregating $20,000 each, and every want abundantly provided for by careful and competent merchant buyers. Our merchants universally are enterprising and competitive, which gives to the consumer a good market in which to buy (Telluride and San Miguel County, 1894).*

Still smarting over Telluride's sole church, community stalwarts explained:

> *The fact that any given place has a multiplicity of churches does not necessitate that it is a specially religious community: very often it is quite the opposite, and conversely the statement that Telluride has only one church does not necessarily imply that we are, for that reason, irreligious, but it does show, and that to our credit, that we are not stupidly and doggedly denominational (Telluride and San Miguel County, 1894).*

An organized and efficient volunteer fire department often made the difference between life and death for hastily constructed mining camps. Moreover, in the late nineteenth-century fire departments constituted sources of community pride and pillars of defense against the ever present danger of a cataclysmic fire — especially in mining towns built primarily of wood. Fourth of July celebrations inevitably found firemen from differ-

Telluride firemen, probably volunteers, stand erect for a photograph in front of the American House on Colorado Avenue. (Telluride Historical Museum)

ent mining towns competing against one another. A city with a championship hose cart team could take comfort in knowing that they had the best fire protection possible.

A group of traveling variety-theatre performers raise a toast for the photographer. (Denver Public Library, Western History Department)

Regional newspapers proved influential in remote mining camps like Telluride because they constituted the sole source of information for many of their loyal readers. Publishers of these provincial publications often slanted the news to reflect their particular political biases — a practice not unheard of today. *The Telluride Journal* legitimately claimed to be the "Oldest Paper in San County." The *San Miguel Examiner* chronicled local happenings for the news-hungry population between 1897 and 1929.

Of course several Telluride businesses catered to the needs of the miners. Along East Pacific Avenue, one block south of Colorado Avenue, miners could have their choice of the illegal and immoral. An eyewitness wrote about miners' weekends in Telluride:

> *What they wanted was easily available . . . . Large combination saloon and gamblings halls (with some restaurants — all with a free lunch) ran twenty-four hours a day and three hundred and sixty-five days a year . . . . Equally well patronized were the Silver Bell and White House dance halls; big houses called the Pick and Gad and the Big Swede's; and the cribs, a series of small shacks each with one female occupant. The big "houses" were the "class" of the red light district. Here, the girls acted more lady-like but not more modest. They were dressed in somewhat fashionable garb, peddled to them in the afternoons by a respected clothing establishment* (Belsey, 1962).

One of the "big houses," the Silver Bell still stands (although little remains of the original structure) on the corner of Pacific Avenue and Spruce Street:

> The original building was constructed in the 1880s and at first consisted of a two-story place called McPhersons' Rooming House, which adjoined the Silver Bell Saloon. On July 4, 1890, a disgruntled customer set fire to the Silver Bell, and the rooming house was severely damaged. Using material salvaged from the original structure, Barney Gabardi and a partner rebuilt the structure and ran it as a saloon and gambling hall (Fetter and Fetter, 1979).

Tame in comparison, but arguably more important for the health of Telluride's citizens, the cattle industry thrived as well. Telluride's Board of Trade boasted that:

> The mode of raising cattle in this country has changed from what it was ten years ago. Instead of depending on range feed the entire year, the cattlemen have been preparing feed with which to winter their stock thereby avoiding heavy losses during the winter months . . . . The conclusion that can be clearly reached from a review of the cattle industry of the County, from an experience of ten years past, is that it has been largely profitable to those engaged in it and that there is plainly unfolded before them a future of constantly increasing prosperity (Telluride and San Miguel County, 1894).

These cowboys might have argued that they had not yet become prosperous on their meager wages. (Telluride Historical Museum)

The city fathers also asserted that the county:

Still contains within its borders room and opportunity for the development of a thousand happy and contented homes. It is a section of broad mesas and beautiful valleys, whose fertile soil need but the fructifying touch to become fruitful producers of all the cereal, vegetable or horticultural products know to the temperate zone (Telluride and San Miguel County, 1894).

The Nauman and Courtney studio snapped this uncommon photo of two Plains Indians, who evidently belonged to a traveling dance troop. *(Courtesy of Bill Mahoney)*

Historians readily express their gratitude to early mining-camp photographers who bequeathed to them a treasure trove of historic images. One of the best and most prolific photographers in Telluride was W. J. Carpenter, a landscape and portrait specialist. Many early photographers, like Carpenter, also advertised on the cardboard that backed their images. To prevent early photographic paper from curling, it was usually glued to a piece of cardboard slightly larger than the photograph itself.

Of course the San Miguel Valley would not have seen the Rio Grande Southern, commercial use of alternating electrical current, fire department, gaming halls, cattle industry, photographers, or even Telluride itself, were it not for the high mines in the mountains nearby. They comprised the heart, guts, and pocketbook of all that Telluride was, or ever would be, in the late nineteenth century.

CHAPTER FOUR

The High Mines

By the time most Colorado mining towns saw the gold standard coming, it was too late. During the early 1890s, Colorado politicians did what they could to defeat the powerful eastern "goldbugs," who wanted a gold-backed monetary system. The general economy of the United States was already in the doldrums, and with the steadily declining price of silver on the world market, several of Britain's mints in India closed on June 26, 1893. More nations throughout the world were turning to gold, rather than silver, to back their currency. Even the entire West did not have enough clout in Congress to keep the government buying silver at inflated prices to buoy the bimetallic (silver and gold) monetary system. So, during that fateful July in 1893, when the United States finally repealed the Sherman Silver Purchase Act, the bottom fell out of the price of silver — dropping it to about 60 cents an ounce, less than one-half its value in 1879. Within a week most silver mines in Colorado closed, crippling the economy.

The collapse of silver prices in the early 1890s strikes most people as nothing more than a bit of uninteresting historical fiscal policy. But, consider the implications. In a matter of days in 1893, a change in the United States government's "uninteresting" monetary policy lead to the demise of the Colorado silver-mining industry that had been the envy of the world for nearly two decades. (Even today, few people understand that our species [coins] and paper currency are no longer backed by either silver or gold. Rather, our money has value only in that people are willing to accept it for goods and services. Should people suddenly decide not to accept our money, because it cannot be exchanged for either silver or gold, it could become worthless overnight.)

Yet in the mid-1890s, when most Colorado silver-mining-towns, including the mighty Leadville, found themselves struggling to survive, substantial gold deposits sustained Telluride. In 1894, even business receipts praised Telluride's mineral deposits and high mines:

> This limited space [on the back of a receipt] forbids further mention of individual properties, but enough has been said to show that the mineral bearing area lying within the boundaries of San Miguel County contains many of the most extensively developed and best paying mines in the state. The future contains boundless possibilities (The Cash Grocery).

While such proclamations were unabashed boosterism, the mining production spoke for itself. Between January 1895 and November 1896 the Tomboy Mine alone extracted $1,250,000 of gold ore, half of which was profit.

From the very beginning, San Juan Mountain communities like Telluride, Ames, Rico, Ophir, and Placerville depended on the high mines for continued growth and prosperity. During the 1880s, before the railroad and most of the tramways, the mines depended on the freighters.

Freighters literally brought everything to the mines, including frozen hogs strapped to the backs of pack mules. The Smuggler-Union provides the stunning backdrop in this photo. (Courtesy of P. David Smith)

The great high mines were truly *high* mines. Even today people in sturdy, well-cushioned SUVs can only negotiate the roads to the mines (many of them nestled in basins over 11,000 feet in elevation) during late summer and early fall, after most of the snow has melted. On the way up and down riders gasp as they inch along hair-raising switchbacks blasted into sheer cliffs. For anyone with a even a touch of vertigo or a slight fear of heights, this is not the place to be. For those able and willing to venture to higher mines than the four-wheel drive tracks will take them, the thin mountain air demands slow going, with plenty of huffing and puffing during frequent stops above timberline. That is why it is so astounding to be faced suddenly with the remnants of *massive* sky-high mining complexes like the Tomboy and Smuggler. "How did they get all this stuff up here?" is usually the first question that echoes among the ruins. Followed by the exclamation, from shivering summer tourists, "They stayed up here all the winter!"

Although humans certainly did their share of hauling materials to and from the high mines, animals, and later trams, did the brunt of the transportation work. Among other foods, carefully packed wooden crates contained oranges, bananas, lemons, berries, peaches, eggs, fish, oysters, potatoes, butter, and onions. Tons of fresh fruit from orchards near Grand

Carpenter photographed this group of pack burros loaded with wooden crates. (Denver Public Library, Western History Department)

Junction, Colorado, wound its way up to the mines on the backs of pack animals as well.

Dave Wood claimed a mule was "the only animal for a job like this because, burros were to [sic] dinky and horses to [sic] flighty." Of the long train below Wood's daughters wrote, "One slip — one mule lost — and the whole train could be lost. But these were men who planned to avoid that first lost mule, and they got the train safely to the mine. The feat is still a favorite story of old-timer yarnsters in Telluride."

From his horse Dave Wood carefully watched the beginning of his cable-connected mule train's legendary trek to the Nellie Mine perched 11,900 feet above sea level. (Courtesy of Dorothy P. Evans)

The Rio Grande Southern cut into the long-haul business of freighters like Dave Wood, but not the short haul. Rather, railroads transferred the supplies directly to freight teams waiting at the Telluride depot. From there beasts of burden transported the goods to where no railroad could go — to the high country mines.

Trailing timbers up to the Tomboy Mine near Telluride. (Courtesy of JoAnn Leech)

Lest one get the impression that negotiating this trail was easy, read the words of Muriel Wolle, well-known chronicler of Colorado mining history in the 1940s:

> *The road [lower Tomboy and Smuggler trail] was literally hung to the cliff, which swept down hundreds of feet to the New Smuggler mill at Pandora. To go ahead was terrifying, to look below sickening. For the first time in my "mining career" I lost my nerve as I thought of driving out onto that hanging road over so much empty space . . .* (Wolle, 1949).

The Tomboy Mine was one of the biggest and best of the high mines. Purchased in 1891 by a syndicate in Shanghai, China, the Far Eastern owners "proceeded to equip [sic] with a power and reduction plant. A large mill building was erected and fitted up with crusher, compound rolls, Huntington mills, vanner and bumping tables for concentration."

> *Just under the peak of the mountain ridge separating Ouray from San Miguel County, in Elephant Basin on Savage Fork of Marshall Creek, lie the properties known as the Belmont and Tomboy lode claims belonging to this company . . . being one of the largest and richest gold mines in the entire San Juan.*

The Tomboy Gold Mining Complex in the summer and winter. (Both courtesy of Irene R. Visintin and Elvira F. Visintin Wunderlich)

The direct current electrical power has been abandoned as inefficient and in its stead is now being installed an alternating current plant that will be supplied with power by the San Miguel Consolidated. Additional ground is being opened up on the mines, and by the time this pamphlet is in the hands of the reader the mill will be running to its full capacity night and day.

All the foregoing quotes are from The Board of Trade's 1894 pamphlet, *Telluride and San Miguel County*, that should have included the following rubric, "Nunn's Power Plant at Ames Saves the Tomboy." In 1897 the Tomboy changed hands again, this time "when it was reported sold to Rothchilds' of London for $2,000,000" (Wolle, 1949).

Two basins north, the mighty Smuggler-Union mining complex rivaled the Tomboy in size and production:

Within the area bounded on the north by Ouray County, on the east by San Juan County, on the south by Dolores County and on the west by Mt. Wilson, whose stern and rugged peak marks the termination of the Continental Divide in that direction is found the world famed Smuggler-Union property, from which since 1879 has been taken more than ten millions [sic] in gold and silver, and that in 1892 produced in gold alone — one-fiftieth — or two percent of the entire gold product of the United

Pictured here is the Smuggler-Union mill tucked beneath Marshall Basin, almost 2,000 feet below the mines. Ingram and Bridal Veil Falls highlight the magnificent mountain backdrop. (Courtesy of P. David Smith)

States. The property of underground work in shafts, levels and tunnels . . . . In its many stopes, levels, up-raises and shafts 1,000 men could find employment, and it would require their constant labor for ten successive years to work out the ore now in sight (Telluride and San Miguel County, 1894).

Marshall Basin is located about four miles northeast of Telluride at altitudes between 11,500 and 12,500 feet. Between 1875 and 1876, the Mendota, Sheridan, Smuggler, and Union (later a part of the Smuggler) were staked close together in Marshall Basin. Indeed, a common vein ran beneath them. "This mineral deposit would turn out to be the largest vein in the district, about four to six feet wide. It was eventually worked for a length of four miles and to a depth of 3,000 feet. In the early years, this vein was called the Sheridan vein, but later, it was usually called the Smuggler-Union" (Collman and McCoy, 1991).

A string of freight animals from the Smuggler-Union, dwarfed by the surroundings, snakes down the Marshall Basin trail. Long wooden snowsheds cover the entrance to the Penn Tunnel. (Walker and Southwest Collection, Center of Southwest Studies, Fort Lewis College)

By the 1890s the Smuggler-Union (and the Tomboy) looked like small cities in the sky. They had enough living accommodations and shelters to keep operating all winter. Historian David Lavender (1987) noted that hundreds of men lived in bunkhouses and ate well in the boarding house. Mining companies knew that good food helped reduce turnover rates. That did not mean, however, that all was well with the miners.

Freighters and their animals take a break in the early 1890s on their way to the Smuggler-Union. Note the man sitting on the boiler and the piece of wheeled machinery being dragged by plow horses. (Reprinted from Telluride and San Miguel County, *1894)*

The Smuggler's boardinghouse with its spacious porch can barely be seen above the Bullion Tunnel, the main access to the rich Smuggler vein. (Walker and Southwest Collection, Center of Southwest Studies, Fort Lewis College)

For three dollars a day, minus a dollar for boarding, miners worked ten-hour shifts, day and night:

> *At the close of the Saturday day shift, workers who were free could go to town, if they wished, and enjoy Telluride's numerous obliging fleshpots. Orders for riding horses were sent to the packers, who led the saddled animals up on that day's trip. The miners whipped the rented mounts back down the hill at a faster pace than was always safe. Late on Sunday they rode back with their hangovers* (Lavender, 1987).

These miners from the Smuggler-Union are mostly young men. Some have candles protruding from their pockets even though electrical lights had long been a fixture at the mine. (Walker and Southwest Collection, Center of Southwest Studies, Fort Lewis College)

Discovered in 1876 at the head of Cornet Creek by an early prospector, W. L. Cornett, the Liberty Bell remained dormant for almost two decades. After the silver collapse of 1893, however, gold ruled. And gold is what the Liberty had. Two years after the turn of the century, its rocky bowels yielded 67,439 tons of gold-bearing ore for an average net profit of $1.62 a ton. That amounted to $109,251 in tax-free profit. Unfortunately, the Liberty Bell is remembered more for its tragedies (see page 49) than its gold.

Freighters were often justifiably described, as they have been here, as the life lines to the mines. Yet one seldom reads about another, equally vital means of conveyance: tramways. Also called "aerial tramways," or simply "trams," these overlooked and under appreciated marvels of engineering merit a prominent place in Telluride mining history. "The upper cable (at the top of the towers) was a fixed cable. The buckets were fitted with a frame and wheels, which rode on this fixed cable. The lower cable was the moving cable and pulled the ore buckets" (Collman and McCoy, 1991).

12094. LIBERTY BELL MINE, WEST TELLURIDE, COLO.

In this spectacular view the Liberty Bell mining complex clings precariously to the steep slopes far above Telluride. (Author's collection)

Snow encroaches on a pair of wooden towers along the lower portion of an incredible 6,700-foot tram constructed from the Smuggler-Union Mill at Pandora to the mine almost 3,000 vertical feet above. (Courtesy of Bill Mahoney)

Despite a century of winter perils, the grand apex tower on the Black Bear Mine stands proudly to this day, a work of art at 12,000 feet. (Courtesy of Bill Mahoney)

Trams transported more than ore. They carried anything that could be heaped, jammed, or wedged into their flat-bottomed buckets. Food, nails, wood, wire, coal, sinks, heaters, bottles, boots, chairs, typewriters, and anything else needed for the operation of the high mines swayed up the cable in rusting brown buckets. Miners also came to and from work in the rhythmically bobbing buckets. Some loved to ride the tram, others abhorred it — especially in winter.

During winter and late spring, avalanches wreaked havoc on the trams. In just seconds hurtling masses of snow smashed towers into splinters, then scattered the pieces down the mountain. To protect towers in well-known slide areas, miners built large stone structures to deflect the powerful and dangerous slides.

Precious little information remains about the hundreds of men who worked small claims scattered throughout the San Juan Mining District, but numerous photographs get the point across. On the bottom of page 38 a group of unidentified miners and a small boy pose by a water flume and crude sluice. They appear to be working the dirt at a fairly low elevation. Another photograph (right) offers a rare glimpse inside a mine shaft. The caption on the front of this photograph reads, "Bottom of air raise & ore chute, 4 level Tidal Wave, Ophir

(Courtesy of P. David Smith)

Colo." The man in the center most likely holds a sack of ore samples. Moving candles created bright, squiggly traces on this old photograph.

What many people do not know is that Telluride's dramatic high mines, which inevitably garnered the most attention, depended on the smelting industry for their survival. Twenty-four hours a day the constant, dull pounding from the Smuggler-Union mills in Pandora could be heard throughout downtown Telluride. Up close the din was deafening. In 1907 Esther Tallman wrote, "We went through the mills where there were sixty stamps working at once, and so much noise! Why you could not even hear your own voice! I don't understand the stamps well enough to describe them better, but I do know they were noisy!" After the old mill and cyanide plant burned in 1920, the Gray Mill that replaced it had no stamps to pound.

The sound of the mill stamps could be called "The Heartbeat of Telluride" during the boom days. (Walker and Southwest Collection, Center of Southwest Studies, Fort Lewis College)

Today tourists and four-wheel-drive devotees flock to Telluride during the late summer and early fall to view the fast-vanishing skeletal remains of these fascinating and spectacular high mines. The exhilaration of negotiating the precipitous roads and the unparalleled mountain vistas are also part of the appeal.

So what happened to Telluride's once-booming mining industry? It obviously did not thrive, let alone survive, as was so confidently predicted by local pundits in the late nineteenth century.

The automobile arrived in Telluride almost as quickly as in the rest of the United States. (Telluride Historical Museum)

CHAPTER FIVE

Problems in Paradise

Telluride resident Martin G. Wenger recalled that on the advent of the new century, his brother and father had "secured some short pieces of three inch pipe and loaded them with sticks of dynamite. They took these to a field about a block from town in preparation of setting off the loud blasts as part of . . . an experience that only one generation of people would live to see . . . the 'Turn of the Century.'" Wenger described what he witnessed as a young boy, "At midnight, pandemonium broke loose. Blasts of dynamite on the mountains sides, shootings of pistols, the church bells and the old fire department bells were rung and the mill whistles were blown for about an hour. It impressed me very much" (Wenger, 1978).

Telluride's boisterous twentieth-century start set the tenor for the first decade of the new century. The businesses supplied the mines, the mines supplied the ore, the mills crushed it, and the Rio Grande Southern Railroad shipped it. A government publication entitled *All About Colorado* (1913) reported that in 1912 San Miguel County produced $2,400,000 in gold, $717,038 in silver, $339,270 in lead, $251,860 in zinc, and $143,000 in copper.

Life was good for the mine owners and prosperous businessmen who walked the wooden boardwalks in fine clothes, smoked expensive cigars, danced the night away at gala balls in Denver, and vacationed in Europe. But these symbols of affluence belonged only to the privileged few. Meanwhile, trouble brewed below.

Most underground miners earned less that the expected $3.00 for a ten to twelve-hour day of backbreaking labor. "Outside" or "surface laborers" were lucky to earn $2.50 for a ten-hour day, while mill workers brought home $4.00 for a twelve-hour shift. There were few, if any, benefits. Since most miners paid for room and board, they ended up in debt to the company. It gets worse. Even though the miners risked their lives daily, few miners owned even a single share of stock in the company. "Big money people" from back East held most of the shares. Moreover, only the shareholders and owners profited from the miners' hard work.

A witness to this as a young boy, local George Belsey (1962) recalled:

> They [miners] were paid $3.00 per day (some, but not many, got more), and they paid $1.00 per day for board and bunk. By modern standards, by any standards, they led a bleak and dangerous life . . . . A few, very few, had families living in town. Welshmen, Irish, Finlanders, Swedes, Italians and Greeks. Predominantly foreigners.

Although they lacked formal education, miners had little trouble comprehending that their dangerous daily drudgery enriched only the already wealthy mine owners. As years passed, resentment among the miners intensified. Finally, these abominable conditions led a group of Telluride miners to join the militant Western Federation of Miners on July 28, 1896. It was time to improve working conditions and time to share the wealth. Still, during the next several years little progress in either domain ensued.

When the owners introduced the fathom system (meaning wages were based on the number of six-foot cubes of ore a miner could extract in a day), the Smuggler-Union men had had enough. They wanted nothing to do with this fathom system, the equivalent of factory piecework but with bodies of ore. The miners went on strike in early May 1901.

Telluride pallbearers pose for the camera while the rest of the funeral procession waits in the background. (Courtesy of Louis and Florence Adreattta Collection)

In a pattern that was to become familiar in several San Juan mines over the next few years, the owners brought in nonunion replacement workers (derisively dubbed "scabs" by the unions). Friction immediately mounted between striking union men and scabs. In this tense atmosphere in November 1901 a load of hay mysteriously caught fire at the mouth of the Smuggler-Union. The billowing smoke and intense heat was quickly sucked deep into the mine, while on the surface the fire spread rapidly. The sequence of events that followed remains controversial, but no one can dispute that the Smuggler-Union tunnel was ruined, the boardinghouse burned to the ground, and twenty-eight men died. A horrifying disaster.

There also continued to be too many funerals among the miners:

> *Death was common at the mines and often grisly. At those altitudes pneumonia was nearly one hundred percent fatal for those who*

contracted it. Men fell down shafts, loose boulders sometimes caved in on them from stope roofs. A driller might set off, in his own face, dynamite that had failed to explode when the preceding shift had fired its rounds (Lavender, 1987).

More insidious forms of death also stalked the miners. "At the Alta [Mine], mercury poisoning, resulting in loss of teeth or even death, was a turn-of-the-century hazard that fueled the crises at the mines" (Fetter and Fetter, 1979).

As a young boy, Martin G. Wenger (1978) witnessed the labor strife. He recalled:

> *Very significant labor trouble occurred in the early 1900s . . . . They reached such proportions that before it was over the State Militia was called in to maintain peace and order . . . . The first strike was called in May 1901 and was followed by much bickering on the part of both the company and the union. Nothing really was accomplished and the Smuggler resumed operations in June. By July 1, William Barney, a non-union supporter and shift boss had disappeared. The union was suspected by many of the Telluride inhabitants to have done away with him. On the 3rd about 250 well-armed union miners surrounded the building and workings of the Smuggler-Union Mine. When the non-union miners came to work, firing broke out and the non-union men fired back and retreated to the Bullion Tunnel [three men died and six were wounded]. The non-union men surrendered their arms on the condition they would not be molested or harmed. That afternoon the*

Dashing Bulkeley Wells (second from right) is shown here with a group of National Guard officers. (American Heritage Center, University of Wyoming)

> *Union men lined up the non-union miners, beat some and took their shoes. They marched them over Imogene Pass to Ouray, telling them never to come back.*

Almost immediately, Wenger recalled, other mines went out on strike. By July 4th an agreement, the equivalent of a modified treaty, had been reached. But neither side was satisfied.

Local lore has held that on July 4, 1903, Telluride's attention turned to Presidential candidate William Jennings Bryon who repeated his famous "Cross of Gold" speech on a grandstand in front of the New Sheridan Hotel. The eloquent Bryan wanted "free silver."

The crowd listens to Presidential candidate William Jennings Bryan at the Sheridan Hotel. (Fort Lewis College, Center of Southwest Studies)

In the early 1900s this silver vs. gold controversy inflamed passions not felt in America since the Civil War. A year earlier another presidential candidate, Socialist Eugene Debs, pled his case in the Sheridan Opera House.

The next few years produced sporadic outbreaks of violence between miners and mine owners. The union directed much of its venom toward Arthur Collins, manager of the Smuggler, who instituted the hated "contract," or "fathom," system. Wenger (1978) relates:

> *Contract mining involved the letting of private contracts to miners, individuals or groups who were paid according to the amount of work done, instead of regular wages. These contractors had to purchase all their supplies from the mining company and could work as many hours as they wished. The Union disagreed with this sys-*

tem because they said the prices paid on the contracts were lowered when soft ground was encountered but not increased when harder rock was struck.

The union men also loathed purchasing equipment and supplies at inflated prices from the company.

The interior of the Telluride Beer Hall included spittoons, a slot machine, and a dog. (Courtesy of Irene R. Visintin and Elvira F. Visintin Wunderlich)

In 1903 Telluride found itself faced with a larger and more violent strike. The miners' union demanded, among other things, $4.50 for an eight-hour day. The owners patently rejected such "absurd" demands, and hired "scabs" to replace the striking men. Tempers flared. Soon bloody fighting threatened anarchy. By order of Colorado's Governor James H. Peabody, who strongly favored the mine owners, hundreds of state militia (also known as the National Guard) arrived in Telluride to protect the strike breakers. To ward off more bloodshed, union troublemakers were herded into a makeshift metal stockade on Colorado Avenue, then ignominiously shipped out on the Rio Grande Southern.

In a futile attempt to prevent these same "union troublemakers" from sneaking back into Telluride, the militiamen stationed themselves in a small, hastily constructed, shelter on top of Imogene Pass, over 13,100 feet above sea level. Union workers facetiously dubbed this grayish rock shelter "Fort Peabody." Remnants of this infamous structure still stand. "In those days every citizen, including the preacher, had a Colt and a Winchester" (Belsey, 1962). A description with the bottom photograph on page 46 reads, "Local citizens and mine owners requested Colorado National Guard to control the streets from September 1, 1903 to November 29, 1904, during strikes by the Western Federation of Miners and United Mine Workers of America."

"Fort Peabody" was really just a shelter for a guard who was stationed there to keep union men from returning to Telluride. (Courtesy of Arlene Reid)

Before the troops arrived in September of 1903 a Telluride vigilante group, the "Citizens Alliance," had taken the law into its own hands:

> *Quite secretly, at the height of the inflammatory incidents, the men of the town used the cover of night to gather up known [union] agitators and sympathizers including a few merchants. The Citizens Alliance marched this group, maybe sixty of them, to the railroad station and deported them on a special train to the nearest town some fifty miles away* (Belsey, 1962).
>
> *Both the local residents of Telluride and visitors had to have military passes even to appear on the town streets. Everyone was*

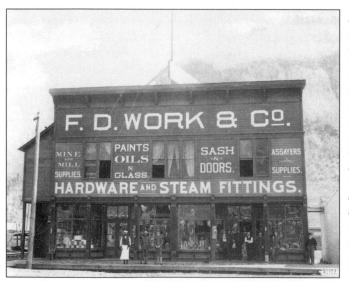

At first glance, one doesn't notice two of Governor Peabody's uniformed National Guardsmen with their rifles, but even the shopkeeper wearing the apron is packing a pistol. (Denver Public Library, Western History Department)

subject to arrest and deportation from the district with hardly any provocation. A resident's house could be searched at any hour of the day or night on nothing more than mere suspicion, or because the owner was thought to be harboring a striking miner or that it might contain a pistol or rifle. More than one Telluride home was left a complete shambles by unruly troopers (Collman and McCoy, 1991).

Bulkeley Wells, another one of Telluride's colorful characters, was born in Chicago and graduated from Harvard as a mining engineer. In 1894, after taking Boston society by storm, the debonair Wells married the elegant Grace Livermore, daughter of millionaire Colonel Thomas Livermore, whose company owned the Smuggler.

Soon after their marriage Wells and his bride moved to Colorado. There he divided his time between Telluride and the even more rarified social atmosphere of Denver. Women found the clever and strikingly handsome Wells irresistible. Indeed, prominent Denver socialite Mrs. Crawford Hill hung a full-length painting of Bulkeley in her mansion.

Bulkeley Wells took over as manager of the Smuggler in 1902, after Arthur Collins was brutally assassinated by a shotgun blast (rumors accused "union men") while sitting in his home in Pandora. Wells unabashedly championed the mine owners and their business interests. Soon he became a captain in the Colorado National Guard.

Martin Wenger (1978) wrote, "Bulkeley Wells greatly impressed me when I was a youngster. I often saw him about town. He had a military bearing and was always dressed immaculately in everyday clothes and when we were attending functions."

Bulkeley Wells, posing as though a Greek god, in his National Guard uniform. (American Heritage Center, University of Wyoming)

Ultimately the influence and money of the mine owners, combined with the power of an arch-conservative governor, prevailed. By 1905 strikes in mining towns across Colorado, including

Telluride, were broken. Miners went back to work for the same low wages, in the same appalling conditions.

From the front porch of her husband's office, Grace Livermore Wells looks into the camera. The mighty Smuggler-Union complex looms in the back-ground. (American Heritage Center, University of Wyoming)

Although she loved Wells, Grace Livermore Wells finally had enough of his long absences and well-known philandering. She divorced him in 1918. Immediately, her father, Robert Livermore, Jr., replaced Wells as manager of the Smuggler.

After the divorce Bulkeley's fortunes plummeted along with the rest of the mining industry. Mining production had been slowly declining since the turn of the century, then came World War I which caused a precipitous drop in ore production. Droves of laborers left the mines to enlist in the military, chemicals became scarce, and the "price of explosives, machinery, freight and smelter services soared, while the value of gold remained fixed by law" (Lavender, 1987). Small mines folded, or so it seemed, daily. In 1928 even the once-mighty Smuggler-Union closed.

Desperately trying to regain his success and wealth, Wells made several ill-advised investments, including a disastrous radium scheme on the Colorado-Utah border. Lavender (1987) observed, "Along the way he married a devoted and gorgeous platinum blonde. At that, Mrs. Crawford Hill reportedly took down his picture from her stair landing," not to mention undermining him financially.

In the early 1900s no one in Telluride would have predicted that this dashing, energetic man would eventually take his own life, rendered unbearable by bad debt and crushed pride. Yet that is what transpired in 1931 when Bulkeley Wells put a gun to his head and pulled the trigger. He was fifty-nine.

As if Telluride's labor troubles in the early 1900s were not enough, nature decided to create even more havoc. Given the tragedies that befell it, it is remarkable that the Liberty Bell showed over $100,000 in profits in 1902. On February 28 a massive snowslide came hurtling down Cornet Creek, taking the Liberty Bell's boardinghouse and some bunkhouses. As rescue teams frantically searched for victims, another slide ran, killing two of the rescuers. Then a third slide let go, sweeping more men to their deaths. By the end of the day sixteen men were dead and ten injured. Some of the bodies were not recovered until spring. That summer lightning struck the Liberty Bell's ore-cart rails, electrocuting three workers deep in the mine.

That the first decade of the new century ended with another natural disaster hardly seemed inappropriate. In 1909 the Trout Lake dam burst, sending torrents of water careening over the San Miguel River banks. Near Ames, the rushing wall of water nearly wiped out Lucien Nunn's alternating-current power plant. Even worse, miles of railroad track between Ames and Placerville were destroyed, isolating Telluride for some time.

Five years later, the big one struck. Cloudbursts in San Juan country, especially in late summer, are nothing unusual. Within minutes creeks rise, rivers rush, bone-dry gulches fill with churning water. Yet on the 27th day of July, 1914, a continuous cloudburst spawned torrential rain. Centered high above Cornet Canyon this torrent of water, after swooping up part of the Liberty Bell Mine waste dump, came crashing down Cornet Creek. It smashed the small dam

One hundred and seventy-five feet of Rio Grande Southern track near Telluride left sixty-two feet in the air by a cloudburst. (Courtesy of Joann Leech)

at the foot of the canyon constructed to divert the creek from its natural course. Gaining momentum, the immense cascade of brownish-gray sludge

Coronet Falls, a short hike from the San Miguel Courthouse. (Reprinted from Telluride and San Miguel County, 1894)

filled with tumbling trees and boulders tore down Oak Street to Colorado Avenue. Terrified residents barely had time to get out of the way. Miraculously, only one fatality occurred. Vera Blakeley dashed back into her home to retrieve her dog, only to be trapped and smothered by debris.

Contorted houses littered the hardest hit residential areas. The force of the surging mass of debris and mud knocked homes off their foundations, twisting and turning them like dollhouses. The surging mass "filled the lower floors of both the Miner's Union Hospital and the Sheridan Hotel with goo, and left a five-foot mass of tangled debris in the central parts of Columbia and Colorado Avenue" (Lavender, 1987).

People must have watched in horror as this beautiful home on North Oak Street twisted off its foundation and nearly fell apart. (Courtesy of P. David Smith)

From the San Miguel Courthouse to the First National Bank, deep, pasty waste inundated Colorado Avenue. (Courtesy of P. David Smith)

Industrious and efficient Telluride miners used powerful fire hoses and a hastily constructed sluice to wash away the deep debris. Few other towns in Colorado could have so quickly garnered the resources and expertise necessary to handle the terrible aftermath of the flood.

The Rio Grande Southern faced more obstacles than floods. Eye-catching scenes like the one pictured meant trouble and extra expense for the struggling railroad. Indeed, the more snow, the more financial headaches. And deep snow in the high San Juans is almost a certainty from December through April. Spring brings even more problems. As the snow melts,

The caption on this postcard states: "Bucking Snow on the Divide near Telluride, Colo. Lizard Head and Mt. Wilson in the distance." (Courtesy of Joann Leech)

meandering creeks become gushing rivers. If the temperature soars suddenly, as they are prone to do in late spring, the snow melt causes the rivers to surge violently over their banks with little or no warning. Railroad bridges wash down stream like twisted match sticks. Once rebuilt, the bridges might only last until fall when they are once again washed out—this time by flash floods caused by enormous cloudbursts.

In the summer many Telluride residents took weekend excurisions to fish, picnic or view the unique geological formation from which Lizard Head took its name. (Courtesy of P. David Smith)

Nor was Telluride spared the suffering and death of the great influenza epidemic in 1918. One out of every ten citizens died during the outbreak. Martin G. Wenger (1978) recalled life in Telluride during this terrible time:

> *The flu epidemic increased by leaps and bounds and the hospital was full. Additional rooms were opened for hospitalizing the miners who were being brought to Telluride each day. There was a shortage of doctors and nurses and many citizens volunteered to act as nurses for the stricken miners.*

A second flu epidemic swept the city in 1919.

Nurses stand on the old Miner's Hospital's front porch. Fully and faithfully restored, it now serves at the Telluride Historical Museum. (Telluride Historical Museum)

Despite all the trouble and a series of new gold discoveries (increasing the supply of the precious metal) in Colorado, Alaska, and South Africa, the largest mines in the Telluride region continued to show a reasonable profit. Zinc obtained from concentrates of the Smuggler-Union brought still more profit, at least to the mine owners. Workers kept improving the roads into the high-country mining basins, better electrified trams shuttled miners and ore alike. A tradition on Christmas Eve, a grand conifer aglow with lights, supplied by power from Lucien Nunn's alternating-current generators, cheered the downtown holiday crowds.

This era, as previously mentioned, also witnessed many of Telluride's young men marching off to join the "war to end all wars." Some did not return. Others came back disillusioned. Prior to Armistice Day, November 11, 1918, the citizens of Telluride held a celebration during which they fashioned a dummy of Kaiser Wilhelm, then burned it in effigy.

On a more personal level, Harriet Fish Backus's classic work, *Tomboy Bride*, is an enjoyable prerequisite (as is Lavender's *One Man's West*) to understanding life in early twentieth-century Telluride. Her words paint a captivating picture of her journey to Telluride, her ascent to the Tomboy, and the excitement and challenge of surviving in a small mining complex impossibly situated in the high San Juans.

By 1920 the heyday of settlement, expansion, and excitement had passed. Telluride settled comfortably into a small mining-town routine. One wonders, however, if the miners and townspeople had any inkling that within two decades most of the mines would be closed and the town largely abandoned.

CHAPTER SIX

Quiet Times

During the 1920s some of the larger mines remained open. The Tomboy Mine complex in Savage Basin comprised a small town complete with post office, heated boardinghouses with running water, a school, and a YMCA (at 12,000 feet surely the highest in America). To the north in Marshall Basin, the Smuggler-Union Mine also boasted many of the amenities of a small town. Down below, Telluride, long since a boom town, kept hoping for better economic times.

History often looks past individuals, yet individuals often reveal much about history. So it is with Ogda Matson Walter and Telluride history during this intriguing, though often overlooked, time period. The youngest of four children, Ogda lived at the Tomboy Mine from 1907 to 1921.

During an interview several years ago, Ogda recalled:

I was born down below, in a house that used to be a crib. We went back up to the mine real soon. Oh, that house, they've moved it

to the city park outside of town. I saw it the other day. Guess they're going to fix it up. [Moved to the east side of Telluride's Town Park, it is now thoroughly refurbished and serves as the Parks and Recreation Department's office.] Many years later my mom, sometime in the '30s, bought a little house for $20 in back taxes. Took her a while to pay it off though. Couldn't buy one for that now.

Before the Matson family encountered hard times, a well-dressed Ogda (front center) holds her sister Elsa's hand. Her other sister, Mildred, and her older brother, Vincent also posed. (Courtesy of Ogda Matson Walter)

She also remembers her father coming home late each evening after working deep in the Tomboy. "His wool socks that my mom knitted for him would be frozen to his legs from all that water down there. It was terrible. No wonder so many of 'em died, just like my dad," she observed without bitterness. "The conditions above ground wasn't so good either," she continued. "In the winter my mom or dad, I can't remember which, strung a rope from our cabin to the schoolhouse. That way in storms and when the wind was blowin' good we could all follow the rope in a line."

In 1923 Ogda Matson started work as a dishwasher at the Sheridan Hotel. She was sixteen. She had little choice. After her father died, her mother moved down to Telluride with her four young children. Mrs. Matson "rubbed her knuckles bare" washing clothes for the "ladies on the line," but she could not earn enough to

The Tennesse Kid gave Ogda this photograph, which he had taken for publicity purposes. (Courtesy of Ogda Matson Walter)

sustain her family. So Ogda dropped out of school and began washing dishes. She earned the going rate of one dollar a day, working eight to nine hours, seven days a week. She received meals and a room in a small six-room boardinghouse, "really just a bed in a room", across the alley behind the hotel. No benefits, no vacations. "When we wanted a vacation we would quit. Then we would come back after a few days and get hired again. But, we knew how to have a good time," Ogda said with a hint of mischief in her voice. "When the Tennessee Kid [who courted Ogda] would take me dancing at

Ogda dressed up as a young girl, complete with doll, for a costume party. (Courtesy of Ogda Matson Walter)

Swede-Finn Hall, I'd get all gussied up at the Personality Shoppe on main street [Colorado Avenue]."

During prohibition the Sheridan Bar served as a lunchroom. In 1928 Ogda married in the Sheridan. The management gave her and her husband a free room on the night of their marriage vows. "Some Sundays before work, or on special holidays, we would go down to the railroad yard and climb on the cars. Mostly we provided our own entertainment. No T.V. or radio back then, you know."

Dressed in their Sunday best, Elsa Matson, Ogda Anderson ("the only other girl named Ogda in Telluride"), Betty Carlson, and Hulda Swan all climbed onto a piece of Rio Grande Southern rolling stock. (Courtesy of Ogda Matson Walter)

Built in 1899, Swede-Finn Hall, where Ogda "danced the night away," still stands at the southeast corner of Townsend Street and West Pacific Avenue. Several lots east, Finn Hall also hosted dances and masquerade balls. Ogda attributed the presence of two halls with similar names, functions, and in such close proximity to "some problems the Finns and the Swedes had getting along." Though proud Americans, Finnish and Swedish workers and their families maintained strong emotional and social ties to their native country.

In the mid-1920s the Telluride Lion's Club Band rode the trails to Rico. There they performed before enthusiastic audiences. During the 1920s Rico's population of approximately 1,000 equaled Telluride's.

The Telluride Lions Club band, shown here in front of the Rio Grande Southern depot in Rico, must have borrowed the Telluride public school's drum. (Courtesy of Arlene Reid)

The Telluride Elks Club baseball team poses for the camera. (Courtesy of Ogda Matson Walter)

Telluride residents kept hoping, and who can blame them, that mining would once again be their salvation. In 1925, a small group of Scandinavian colleagues took a "cleanup lease" on the Black Bear Mine far above Telluride in Ingram Basin (one basin south of Savage Basin). The revival attempt ended abruptly in 1926 when two of the Scandinavians, Ed and Marie Rajala, perished in a avalanche.

Miners' wages didn't seem like much back then, but they were still about the best salaries in the San Juans. A 1923 Smuggler-Union wage scale from Smuggler, Colorado, listed miners' "day wages." The names of the jobs themselves also reveal the elaborate division of labor down in the mines: Stoping Machine Men ($4.50), Leyner Machine Men ($4.75), Timbermen ($4.50), Timber Helpers ($4.00), Chute Blasters ($4.50), Rippers ($4.50), Muckers & Tramers ($4.00), Cagers ($4.00), Ore Sorters ($5.00), Old Stope Miners ($5.10), Motormen ($4.00), Powder Monkeys ($4.25), Shaft Men ($5.50), Track Men ($4.50), Pump Men ($4.25), Pipe Men ($4.25), Hoist Men ($4.75), Compressor Men ($4.50), Samplers ($4.50), Crusher Men ($4.00), Dumpers ($4.00), Yard Men ($3.50), Laborers ($3.50), Watchmen ($4.00), and Shift Bosses ($6.25 and Bonus).

After the Tomboy Mine closed in 1927, manager David Heron asked local miner John Foster if he wanted to be a year-round watchman, and contract miner, at the mine. Since Foster's contract mining business was floundering, he accepted. Foster recorded a visual record of his Tomboy years. He acquired the nickname "Peg Leg" after he lost the lower portion of his left leg at the Little Mary Mill in Pandora. John Grimsby, his grandson, believes the accident occurred while his grandfather was using a pole to shove troublesome rocks into the middle of a crusher. Somehow a wire on one of the large crusher conveyor belts caught Foster's left pant leg, jerking his leg underneath the fast-moving belt, severing it at the knee. Foster recovered from the terrible accident to become a proud mainstay in Telluride's Fourth of July parades, usually with his mule in tow.

Prior to becoming the watchman at the Tomboy, John Foster ordered supplies from Sears and Roebuck in Kansas City, Missouri. He began corresponding with one of the girls who filled his orders. The letters became more serious. Finally, Frances — the ultimate "mail-order bride" — found Foster's letters and the lure of adventure in the San Juan Mountains irresistible. Sight unseen she agreed to marry Peg Leg. Soon after arriving in Telluride, Frances found herself living at the abandoned Tomboy mining complex.

Nothing in Kansas City life could have prepared her for the solitude and challenges she would face in the high San Juans. Yet in many of the photographs, her eyes still twinkled with adventure. Twenty years earlier Harriet Backus described a home similar to this in *Tomboy Bride:*

Our entrance was made of three rotting planks weakly supported by a six-inch-thick log on the down side. Squatted flat on the ground unpainted, like all the other shacks, it measured twenty-two feet by ten feet in size and was built of one-inch boards with battens, but no lining whatever. It was divided into three sections, our parlor and kitchen each eight feet deep, a six-foot sleeping compartment was literally squeezed in. A small window on each side of the front room and one in the

Frances poses happily in front of her company home at the Tomboy. (Courtesy of John Grimsby)

kitchen supplied daylight. The middle or bedroom had no window, but from the middle of its rough ceiling was a long cord and a small electric light bulb which could be carried into the front or back rooms to light the darkness.

There were many covered Tomboy walkways. It protected the miners as they walked between the boardinghouse and the mine. By the time the Tomboy mining complex shut down, it resembled a humongous

marmot colony in winter, with its snowsheds appearing to be many-branched burrows.

John Grimsby recalls that his grandfather and Frances occasionally panned for gold in the waste dumps (also called "tailings"). He explains that early methods for extracting gold from the crushed ore were inefficient, meaning that much of the ore dumped after processing still contained gold. In fact, mining the massive tailings piles soon became serious business in the San Juans.

One can hardly blame a young John Grimsby, however, for being singularly impressed by the

The common notion that snowshoes and skis were strictly utilitarian is challenged by Frances's smiles. (Courtesy of John Grimsby)

Tomboy's abandoned bowling alley. He still vividly recalls sending "wooden discs, not balls" sliding down the alley toward the pins. Surely the world's highest bowling alley.

Unfortunately, Frances suffered psychologically in the extreme isolation, Spartan living conditions, and brutal climate. Most humans found it challenging enough to live at the Tomboy when it was chocked full of miners and families. Thus, by the time John Grimsby visited his

Frances, a friend, and Peg Leg pan for gold in the waste dumps (also called tailings) of the Tomboy Mine. (Courtesy of John Grimsby)

grandfather at the Tomboy in 1935, Frances had gone back to Kansas.

Once the depression set in, Telluride's fortunes took what looked to be a permanent nosedive despite a local banker's illegal scheme to prevent it. Indeed, Telluride struggled to survive after the closure of the Tomboy, Smuggler, and scores of other mines. When the stock market collapsed in 1929, it was too much for the small mining

In 1933, Frances and a friend, in their fashionable leather jackets and jodhpurs, strike confident poses on top of their sporty Chrysler convertible. (Courtesy of John Grimsby)

town. Telluride's population quickly plummeted to less than 600. To prevent a rush of creditors, the Bank of Telluride temporarily closed its doors in September 1929. Hardworking Telluride citizens — like people throughout America — lost their life savings overnight.

The handguns laying on the bank's table were as much for show as security. (Walker and Southwest Collection, Center of Southwest Studies, Fort Lewis College)

Before the Bank of Telluride closed, its colorful and high-profile president, Charles (Buck) Waggoner arranged a visual demonstration of his bank's assets. When it became clear to Waggoner that he could not keep his bank afloat, he concocted a complicated financial scheme that involved defrauding some large New York financial institutions. Some historians claim that Waggoner's financial conspiracy was an effort to repay his friends in town, others say he did it for himself. Two things are certain, Waggoner ended up in jail and the Bank of Telluride finally folded in 1934. Three decades would pass before it opened again.

Barely ten years after the Waggoner scandal, another scandal erupted. Sheriff Lawrence E. Warick arrested a ring of Telluride highgraders — miners who smuggled rich pieces of ore out of the mine. The *Denver Post* reported that the theft of "$50,000 to $100,000 worth of gold" from the Smuggler-Union and the Tomboy made it the "largest highgrading case in the state's history."

By the mid-1930s Telluride's population dropped below 500. Even the priest left town:

Telluride again became a mission of Montrose sixty-five miles
away. There were no paved roads, and no regular mass was held.
The solitude of the 1880s fell upon the town . . . . The Pick &
Gad, Idle House, Big Swede, and the cribs were still open, but the
main street was a far cry from the exuberant days of the
bullwackers, mule trains, and celebrating miners on a binge
(Fetter and Fetter, 1979).

Built in 1896, St. Patrick's Catholic Church stood vacant at the corner of Galena Avenue and North Spruce Street. This section of town became known as "Catholic Hill" because of the large number of Catholic Italians and Austrians who lived there. Refurbished and once again beckoning the faithful, St. Patrick's still stands on its original location on Catholic Hill.

In the 1930s Fourth of July still meant spirited parades and contests in Telluride, no matter how depleted the population or depressed the economy. "Double-jacking" drilling contests proved especially popular. One man wielded an eight-pound sledge while another held the steel drill. "Changing steel" involved pitching a dull drill and quickly replacing it with a smaller, sharper drill without missing a stroke.

During the 1930s and 1940s independent mining contractors arranged to rework old mill tailings. Money could still be made by trucking ore down from the Tomboy to the huge "Red Mill" in Pandora, where refined ore-processing techniques yielded valuable base metals and gold. But ore shipments still decreased significantly during the 1930s and 1940s. The ore shipped from the Great Red Mill usually ended up at large smelters in Durango.

Even with electrical power, the mining industry's appetite for lumber was so voracious that many of the adjacent forests were soon depleted. Cribbing — shoring up mine tunnels and shafts with timber — accounted for a large portion of the timber used. Although not all tunnels were as heavily cribbed as the one shown on page 64, over 350 miles of tunnels in the San Miguel Mining District necessitated a prodigious amount of timber.

Like giant paramecia, toxic tailings ponds from the Pandora mills stretched west toward Telluride. Cyanide, mercury, and other toxic substances permeated these ponds, percolating into the soil and water beneath them. Today this series of poisonous ponds has been reclaimed, meaning the toxic material has been "cleansed." The remains of the pond sites are now covered with grass. And trout once again thrive in the San Miguel River below.

Bootlegging helped Telluride survive during the Great Depression. Tons of sugar was shipped in, legal or not. Despite all the laws and ordinances forbidding the "production or sale" of hard liquor, it flowed freely in several back rooms. Most of the townspeople simply looked the other way.

Pictured here is a heavily cribbed mine tunnel, probably in the late 1940s, in the Smuggler-Union. (Walker and Southwest Collection, Center of Southwest Studies, Fort Lewis College)

They knew Telluride needed bootleg liquor to survive. "Prohibition was stupid anyway," one liberal old-timer rationalized.

To the relief of the townspeople, Dr. Joe Parker arrived in Telluride in 1932. For fifteen years he served as the only medical doctor in the economically depressed Telluride region. By all accounts Joe Parker, who obtained his medical degree from the University of Colorado in 1931, was a fine human, physician, and community leader.

Stories still circulate about many of the challenges he faced. For example, Fetter and Fetter (1979) wrote:

> *The hospital used a form of anesthesia known as the 'drip-mask' method, which used ether dripped onto a piece of folded gauze held over the patient's nose. It was safer than chloroform but not without risk, especially when the power failed. The danger of explosion was too great to use a kerosene lamp, so Dr. Parker rapidly became skilled at performing surgery, delivering babies, and setting fractures in the dark.*

The Argentine Mine in Rico hired Dr. Parker for $400 a month to make a weekly trip to Rico. Each Thursday afternoon he would tend to the medical needs of the mine's 200 employees and their families. Later the Argentine Mine reimbursed Dr. Parker based on a capitation method. For example, each miner would have $1 a month deducted from his salary to pay the doctor's salary. If there were 150 miners employed, the doctor would receive $150. But, the doctor had to pay for all medical supplies. So some months, when few miners needed medicines and supplies, Dr. Parker earned money. Other months, when several miners needed medicines and supplies, Dr. Parker lost money. His son (himself a doctor) points out that this was probably one of the first, and still controversial, medical capitation plans in the United States.

As a gesture of appreciation for all Dr. Parker had done for them, some of the miners in Telluride winched a vacant crib onto a flatbed truck and hauled it up to Trout Lake, located about half way between Telluride and Rico. This provided Dr. Parker with a place to rest during his trips between Rico and Telluride, or to wait out bad weather. He also liked to fish. Today this crib still serves as the Parker family's vacation home.

Toward the end of the 1940s Telluride languished like never before, its population threatening to drop below 400. Even Dr. Parker reluctantly left town in 1947. The locals who remained said that their beloved mountain settlement retained a comforting small-town rhythm. During the summer a few tourists, railroad buffs, and amateur historians visited the remote mining camp. A mine or two might open, some independent contractor might hit a rich pocket or two, and some bad whiskey might send a few imbibers to the hospital. During the winter, however, the town went into a deep freeze. Occasionally indoor bazaars and dinners were held in the high school and the courthouse. Mining activity, even though underground, seemed to subside as well.

Telluride's real boom began in 1891 with the coming of the Rio Grande Southern Railroad. Sixty years later there were only a few hun-

An electric sign advertising a Telluride movie theatre hangs above Harry Miller's barbershop on Colorado Avenue after a big snow. (Courtesy of Ogda Matson Walter and Roger Polley)

dred townspeople left to mourn its demise. After a series of disputes with managers of various Telluride mines, dwindling numbers of tourists, an a debt of $9,000,000 (close to the amount Otto Mears had to raise to get the line running), it folded on September 20, 1951. No longer would

This postcard's caption reads, "The Galloping Goose-unique train on the Rio Grande Southern in Southwestern Colo." (Author's collection)

In forlorn Telluride the Rio Grande Southern's tracks have been torn up and the water tower stands empty. (Denver Public Library, Western History Department)

people hear the whistle of the Rio Grande Southern engines echo throughout the San Miguel Valley. Although the boom had long since passed, the collapse of the Rio Grande Southern solidified the economic disaster that enveloped Telluride.

By the mid-1950s, the few remaining locals felt it was only a matter of time before Telluride, like so many other small Colorado mining towns, would become a ghost town. Soon, they feared, only dilapidated homes and vandalized buildings would remain. That saddened those who clung to life in Telluride, because it was their town, their heritage, and they cherished both.

CHAPTER SEVEN

Snowy Savior

A t the beginning of the twenty-first century, it is hard to imagine Telluride being anything other than a world-class ski resort and summer-tourist Mecca. But Telluride, and all that its unique name conjures up, did not become, well, Telluride, overnight.

After its inception in the late 1870s, Telluride had an incredible economic run. But by the end of the Great Depression in the mid-1930s, it was nearly over. By 1960, it was really over. Although it would have seemed unimaginable to those who experienced the late nineteenth-century boom days, in 1960 barely 500 people called Telluride their home. The mining gods had finally and completely deserted this beautiful mountain town. Plus, it is a safe bet that only a very few Telluride residents in the 1960s could have imagined that the floundering town's economic salvation lie in snow.

Snow, Telluride's savior? From the moment the first prospector set foot in the valley, snow had been the enemy. Prospectors abhorred it, animals struggled through it, train engines ground to a halt in it, automobiles got stuck in it, merchants cursed it, and roofs collapsed under its weight. That snow could ever be part of the town's economic revival would have struck

In the 1970s Telluride was halfway between a mining town and a ski town, but its jewel-like setting remained the same. (Courtesy of Arlene Reid)

most of the town's residents as the pinnacle of irony. For decades miners had rigged utilitarian wooden skis to travel from one place to another. Indeed, for over a half century residents enjoyed utilitarian skiing in the Telluride vicinity. Admittedly, on rare occasions they swooped and hollered their way down steep slopes, but how could there be any money in that?

Robert Livermore poses with a friend on skis about 1900. Simple leather straps acted as bindings and a long pole was used to push and steer. (American Heritage Center, University of Wyoming)

As for skiing being a sport, or major tourist attraction, some of the kids in the 1930s and 1940s enjoyed trudging up the surrounding hills, then skiing back down. Sometimes locals, like Alta Cassietto, would "even haul their seven-foot wooden skis to the more gently sloped Dallas Divide area." Then in the late 1930s, Bruce Palmer, a man from Austria, rigged a rope tow on the snowy slope of Grizzly Gulch near downtown Telluride. At first a few locals used this novel towing device at their convenience. Later, one could join the newly formed Ski-Hi Club for five dollars a season. Soon the club extended the length of the tow to 1,500 feet. It even staged a few races that attracted contestants from nearby towns. During the early 1940s, with World War II raging, the tow rope still continued to ferry a few Telluride children and adults up the gulch. Even after World War II, however, no one in the West, save a few dreamers in nascent Aspen, Colorado, thought much about the economic implications of recreational skiing.

In the late 1930s, Telluride resident and author, Martin G. Wenger, unknowingly became part of local skiing history. When the late Martin G. Wenger learned that his younger brother, Herbert, was a "bit down and out," he invited him to work his unpatented Zulu claim during the summer. The name "Zulu" came to Martin many years earlier while reading a book about Africa. Martin's son, Martin Jr., also spent his summer breaks helping his uncle work the mine. They lived in a tiny one-room cabin from May through September for several summers.

Telluride skiing in the 1960s consisted of this rope tow in Grizzly Gulch near downtown. (Courtesy of Arlene Reid)

Their mine was located high above Telluride and the only persons they saw were "United States Geological Survey employees and a power-line walker." Martin's son recalled that about once a month "they would hike to town and rent a horse to haul up supplies." They obtained water by melting portions of a big snowdrift. Now, every winter thousands of people ski down "Zulu Queen," where the Wenger cabin once stood.

By the mid-1940s, caravans of skiers' cars lined the summit of Dallas Divide between Telluride and Ridgway. Among some of those early Dallas-Divide ski devotees were Dr. Joe Parker and, as one might expect, Bruce Palmer. The more skilled had fun jumping adroitly over a barbwire fence near the base of the long, gentle run.

During the 1950s and 1960s not much happened in backwoods Telluride. Although by

In 1938 Bruce Palmer flies through the air with the greatest of ease. A visual metaphor for Telluride's ultimately soaring success. (Courtesy of Bill Mahoney)

the late 1960s and early 1970s, "hippies," or "flower children," slowly and unobtrusively drifted in from around the United States. Attracted by Telluride's pristine setting, geographic isolation, and low-cost— though largely dilapidated — housing, they happily "did their own thing." Surely few of the old-timers, let alone the laid-back newcomers, suspected that another economic boom would soon come barreling down the mountains.

New technologies, America's changing leisure patterns following World War II, and the skiing craze that ran wild through the Rockies in the late 1960s and early 1970s, contributed significantly to Telluride's revival and current dizzying success. That tourists also started to flock to Telluride during the summer months, for festivals and intellectual gatherings, seemed only natural. What better place to stage festivals or discuss intellectual issues than in a invigorating mountain environment — far away from the daily mind-numbing responsibilities and minutia? Anyone who has hiked along an untrammeled stretch of mountain stream, meandered through an alpine meadow flush with flowers, or sat on top of a mountain ridge amid indescribably natural grandeur knows that special, all-too-rare feeling of outdoor bliss. So too, summer recreational opportunities abounded in the San Miguel Valley region. Skiing, however, would come to reign supreme.

Suddenly, in the early 1970s, it was the scale and purpose of skiing that changed dramatically:

> *Promoters went among the peaks like old-time mineral prospectors, hunting for rich strikes. One who came to Telluride and immediately grasped its potentials was Joseph T. Zoline of Beverly Hills, who had discovered the magic of ski development at Aspen. You built lifts and runs, at a loss if necessary, to bring people into an area, and then you sold them, at high prices, real estate on which to build winter homes"* (Lavender, 1987).

In other words, those *with* money had the only chance — much like the mining capitalists of a century ago — to earn even *more* money. So it was to be with Telluride. Resident miner and avid local historian Bill Mahoney, a member of the Colorado Ski Hall of Fame, oversaw the development of Joe Zoline's now famous Telluride ski area in the 1970s.

Although the "hippie element" did not welcome the changes, there was nothing they could do to stop them. More and more winter tourists arrived with trendy ski clothes, equipment, and lots of money to spend. Many of them wanted vacation homes in this idyllic valley. So prices for houses and buildings in town, *any* houses and buildings, moved swiftly higher. Condominiums sprouted like wild flowers in spring. What little open space remained on the constricted floor of the San Miguel Valley increased even

Bill Mahoney, who oversaw the development of the Telluride Ski area in the 1970s. (Courtesy Telluride Magazine, Doug Berry photograph)

more rapidly in value. In the nearby foothills, ranches traded hands as developers competed for what little flat space remained available. By the 1980s and 1990s, with the ski areas and summer festivals going full tilt, most of the more laid-back element had simply drifted out of town, just as they had drifted in.

What some people do not realize is that this so-called "hippie element" left an indelible cultural impression on Telluride. On a small scale their legacy includes the "free-box" in town, where one can select discarded clothes and who-knows-what else, and a quaint popular bakery. On a larger scale, the free spirit of these so-called hippies lives on in Telluride's astounding array of festivals. These include, among numerous others, the Blue Grass Festival, Mountain Film Festival, Blues and Brews Festival, Chamber Music Festival, Jazz Festival, the internationally renowned Film Festival, and, more directly to the point, the Mushroom Festival. And consider the Ah Haa School for the Arts and the Faraway Foundation that "emphasizes the human relationship to the natural world, to self, and to others." Of course one should not forget that the music of The Grateful Dead echoed throughout the San Miguel Valley several times. A 2002 front-page story in the *Denver Post* described a "Holy Man" who helped rid the city council chamber of malevolent spirits. Only in Telluride.

The rest is history. Telluride and its newer companion, Mountain Village, continue to thrive. The permanent population once again approaches 2,500. Hundreds, sometimes thousands, of people visit Telluride and Mountain Village daily. Several thousand more well-heeled tourists take up temporary residence during the winter ski season and the summer festival season. The town's Web site informs one that, "Telluride shares the same latitude as San Francisco and Athens, Greece," and that, "Telluride and Mountain Village offer the best of Colorado's past and progressive present. A National Historic Landmark District with Victorian-era architecture, Telluride rests at the base of the Telluride Ski Mountain and is surrounded by 13,000-foot (almost 4,000 meters) peaks. Telluride is connected to Mountain Village by a free gondola. Located mid-mountain at 9,500 feet above sea level, Mountain Village overlooks some of Colorado's most magnificent peaks."

Wonder what else you can do in the Telluride

Now a fast-moving, modern gondola whisks tourists, skiers, and snowboarders to the newer Mountain Village and the ski slopes above Telluride. (Author's photograph)

region besides ski and attend festivals? All you have to do is double-click on any of the following, assuming you are looking at the Telluride Web site: BIKING, CAMPING, CLIMBING, FISHING, FOR KIDS, GLIDER RIDES, GROUP RETREATS, HIKING, HISTORY, HORSE RIDES, ICE CLIMBING, ICE SKATING, INDOOR ACTIVITIES, KAYAKING, OUTFITTING, RAFTING, SKATEBOARD RAMP, SLEIGH RIDES, SNOWMOBILING, SNOWSHOEING, SWIMMING, TOURS, TOWN PARK, ULTRA LIGHT, and among others, YOUTH CENTER.

Along with the beauty of the surrounding mountains and the town's 8,750 foot altitude, home and land prices now take one's breath away as well. Upscale condominiums abound, a massive luxury hotel boasts a championship golf course, and clusters of pricey shops tempt the wealthy. An airport runway, that avoids all the trials and tribulations of a mountain railroad, welcomes more visitors every year. Of course spas and gourmet restaurants abound. In downtown Telluride Victorian-era homes are beautifully refurbished and an inviting new library beckons the more literary. The faithfully restored old Miner's Hospital building now serves as the Telluride Historical Museum. It features a wonderful cornucopia of intriguing displays and relics.

An original tram tower airlifted from the high country down to the base of the mountain serves as a reminder of the gondola's high-country mining legacy. (Author's photograph)

So it is no surprise that many of the world's most famous and rich frequent Telluride. They rub shoulders in gorgeous, opulent homes while taking in some of the most beautiful vistas in America. The skies are bright and the stars twinkle at night. Welcome to Shangri-la. Welcome to Telluride. And by the way, the boom days are back.

Lest we forget, however, history gently reminds us that in this region, mining once reigned absolutely supreme, then disappeared. Although today it seems unimaginable, the current kings, skiing and festivals, may someday disappear from the San Miguel Valley as well. No matter, the essence of Telluride lies in the majestic beauty that encompasses it. As long as that essence is not completely compromised, Telluride will survive.

Bibliography

Adams, E. B. (date unknown). *Gio Oberto of Telluride, Colorado.* Grand Junction, Colorado: Private printing. (Courtesy of Dr. Jim Parker)

Backus, H. F. (1969). *Tomboy Bride.* Boulder, Colorado: Pruett Publishing Company.

Bailey, S. A. (1933). *L. L. Nunn, a Memoir.* Ithaca, New York: Cayuga Press.

Belsey Jr., G. W. (1962). "When to Telluride, to Helluride!" Unpublished manuscript. (Courtesy of Alta Cassietto).

Brown, R. L. (1968). *An Empire of Silver.* Caldwell, Idaho: Caston Printers, Ltd.

Buys, C. J. (1986). "Power in the Mountains: Lucien Nunn Catapults the San Juans into the Age of Electricity." *Colorado Heritage,* Volume 4, 25 - 37.

Buys, C. J. (1993). "Fort Crawford: A Symbol of Transition." *Journal of the Western Slope,* Volume 8 (2), 1 - 29.

Buys, C. J. (1997). *Historic Leadville in Rare Photographs and Drawings.* Ouray, Colorado: Western Reflections.

Buys, C. J. (1998). *Historic Telluride in Rare Photographs.* Ouray, Colorado: Western Reflections Publishing.

Buys, C. J. (1999). *Illustrations of Historic Colorado.* Ouray, Colorado: Western Reflections Publishing.

Buys, C. J. (Summer 2000). "'Mothers Rushed into the Deluge': Telluride's Great Flood of 1914." Colorado Heritage, 2 - 13.

Buys, C. J. (2002). *The Lost Journals of Charles S. Armstrong, From Arkport, New York to Aspen, Colorado — 1867 - 1894.* Western Reflections Publishing: Montrose, Colorado.

Collman, R., and McCoy, D. A. (1991). *The R. G. S. [Rio Grande Southern] Story: Volume II — "Telluride, Pandora, and the Mines Above".* Denver, Colorado: Sundance Publications, Ltd.

Crofutt, G. A. (1881). *Crofutt's Grip-Sack Guide of Colorado.* Omaha, Nebraska: Overland Publishing Company.

Crofutt, G. A. (1885: 1981 reprint). *Grip-Sack Guide of Colorado.* Boulder, Colorado: Johnson Publishing Company.

Crum, J. M. (1954: 1961 reprint). *The Rio Grande Southern Railroad.* Durango, Colorado: San Juan History (Hamilton Press).

Fetter, R. L., and Fetter, S. (1979: 1990 reprint). *Telluride, "From Pick to Powder."* Caldwell, Idaho: Caxton Printers.

Gibbons, Rev. J. J. (1898: 1987 reprint). *In the San Juans: Sketches.* Telluride, Colorado: Private printing.

Gregory, M., and Smith, P. D. (1984). *Mountain Mysteries: The Ouray Odyssey*. Ouray, Colorado: Wayfinder Press.

Lavender, D. (1943: 1977 reprint). *One Man's West*. Lincoln, Nebraska: University of Nebraska Press.

Lavender, D. (1964). *A Rocky Mountain Fantasy, Telluride, Colorado*. Telluride, Colorado: San Miguel County Historical Society.

Lavender, D. (with photography by G. H. H. Huey). (1987). *The Telluride Story*. Ridgway, Colorado: Wayfinder Press.

Ordinances of the City of Telluride. 1917. (1917). Telluride, Colorado: *San Miguel Examiner* (City Council of Telluride).

"Pioneers of the San Juan Country. Vol. I." (1942). By the Sara Platt Decker Chapter of the N. S. D.A.R. of Durango, Colorado. Colorado Springs: The Out West Printing and Stationery Company. (Courtesy of Bill Ellicott).

"Pioneers of the San Juan Country. Vol. III." (1952). By the Sarah Platt Decker Chapter of the N. S. D. A. R. Durango, Colorado: Durango, Colorado.

"St. Patrick's Church, Sixtieth Anniversary, 1896 - 1956, Telluride, Colorado." (1956). Montrose, Colorado: *Montrose Daily Press. (Courtesy of Bill Ellicott)*.

Tallman, R. (1907). Unpublished correspondence. (Courtesy of Dr. James Parker).

Telluride and San Miguel Country, Colorado. (1894). Denver, Colorado: The Publishers Press Room Company (Telluride Board of Trade).

Wagner, Bessie. (date unknown). "A Few Notes about Pioneer Mining in the Telluride, Colorado, Area." Unpublished manuscript. (Courtesy of Bill Mahoney)

Weber, R. (1974). *A Quick History of Telluride*. Colorado Springs, Colorado: Little London Press.

Wenger, M. G. (1978: 1989 reprint). *Recollections of Telluride Colorado: 1895 - 1920*. Durango, Colorado: Private Printing.

Western Colorado Power Colorado Collection (Boxes 1 - 5) held by the Center of Southwest Studies, Fort Lewis College, Durango, Colorado.

Wichmann, I. (date unknown). "History of Telluride." Unpublished manuscript. (Courtesy of Alta Cassietto).

Williams' Tourists' Guide and Map of The San Juan Mines of Colorado. (1877). Publishers unknown.

Wolle, M. S. (1949). *Stampede to Timberline*. Boulder, Colorado: Private printing.

Wood, F., and Wood, D. (1977). *"I Hauled These Mountains in Here."* Caldwell, Idaho. Caxton Printers, Ltd.

Wright, A. (1974). "Mining town doctor." *Daily Sentinel*, May 26. Grand Junction, Colorado.

Index